D1483755

PRAISE

If you are not fired up as an educator and leader, you NEED to read this book! Frank Rudnesky's positive energy comes through loud and clear in *Fired Up Leadership.* The easy to read format invites the reader on a journey of self-discovery as a leader, or a renewed commitment to being the leader who walks the talk with their staff by exuding positivity and a team approach. Don't miss this opportunity to get FIRED UP!

Michele Rispo Hill | Passionate Educator
Coordinator of Admissions & Communications

To say that Dr. Rudnesky leads by example, would be an understatement. He has always modeled what leaders should do for their students and Staffulty! I am continually inspired by his books and have read them multiple times. I devoured his new book, Fired Up Leadership. He has filled my bucket and I am ready to take on leading in a positive and *FIRED UP* fashion for many years to come! This is a book that can be used to teach our future leaders, very inspiring!

Dr. Michelle Carney-Ray Yoder | Proud Superintendent
Presenter | Adjunct Professor

Fired Up Leadership propels you from words into action. Through powerful stories, practical exercises, and sound wisdom, Dr. Rudnesky entertains you with his innate passion for not only making people better, but helping them lead from the heart. All of this leads to better schools with students who are empowered and ready to make the world a better place.

Dr. Brandon Beck
Author | Speaker | Educator

Frank does not just simply talk about leadership, he embodies leadership through the way he leads, lives, and most importantly how he serves others. This book is a sneak peek into Frank's life and how his *Fired Up* attitude and effort have allowed him to be one of the most dynamic, influential, and effective school leaders I know. This book is a must-read for all educators! It is guaranteed to get you *Fired Up* for leadership and life!

Mark Brown | Administrator
Speaker | Author, Choose To Be You

Frank is all about helping you and your kids believe that leaders are made, not born. Fired Up Leadership is filled with practical steps, stories, and encouragement to help everyone have the tools necessary to become a leader.

Chris Woods
Educator | Author | Speaker | STEM Nerd

When it comes to leadership in the field of education, it simply doesn't get much better than Dr. Frank Rudnesky. With so many years of experience in leadership development, he has a plethora of ideas, tips, and strategies for maximizing the leadership capacity in students and educators alike. Frank has a knack for challenging the status quo and creating new perspectives, and this book is no exception. You're going to reflect, you're going to relate, and, most importantly, you're going to grow throughout the course of this book. Fired Up Leadership is an absolute grand slam if you are looking to take your leadership skills to the next level!

Dr. Phil Campbell | Educator
Jostens Renaissance Ambassador
Host of The Green Room Podcast Series

You can't help but be "Fired Up" when you read this book. Dr. Rudnesky's reminder to use experiences that shaped us through our lives to define the type of leader we can be, is both insightful and empowering. His encouragement to let our innate character traits, our ability to communicate and listen, our desire to serve, influence our leadership capabilities is empowering. Using team building to empower others and encouraging others to bring solutions to the table, helps when we need to set goals, lead a vision and live out our intentions. Let passion drive you and celebrate along the way! Keep pushing those boundaries!

Melissa Daddabbo | Administrator

The adage, "there is strength in numbers" rings true throughout Frank's words as he strives to build, foster, and grow more leaders. For many years, and to countless people, Frank has served as a trusted advisor and mentor when it comes to leadership and the wisdom shared in Fired Up Leadership will serve everyone in their endeavor to be a better leader and a better person.

Bradlee W. Skinner
Author | Educator | Speaker

From the time that I attended Belhaven Middle School, I learned what true leadership was at a very young age. Dr. R. my middle school principal, always emphasized the importance of gratitude, integrity, and teamwork.

Glenn
Student | Collegiate Athlete

Being a Fired Up Leader is more than just running around with energy and high-fiving people. It takes being intentional and mindful of your leadership steps. Dr. R's 5 Domain approach to leadership will keep leaders of all skill and experience levels focused on the work, the people, and the energy. As one of the very best in the business, Dr R brings with him a belief that everyone has a leader inside them and we need only give them the opportunity to lead. This book will get you FIRED UP!

Dr. Darrin Peppard | Superintendent
Speaker | Author, Road to Awesome

The art of effective leadership involves many facets, but inspiration, motivation, and a passionate message are at its core. Dr. Frank Rudnesky provides just that in "Fired Up Leadership." When reading this book you will be left with thought provoking questions and authentic and relevant tools to keep you fired up as you continue your educational journey.

Jonathan Alsheimer
Educator | Speaker | Author, Next Level Teaching

FIRED UP LEADERSHIP

DR. FRANK RUDNESKY

FIRED UP LEADERSHIP
Copyright © by Dr. Frank Rudnesky
First edition 2020

All rights reserved.

No part of this publication may be reproduced in any form, or by any means, electronic or mechanical, including photocopying, recording, or any information browsing, storage or retrieval system, without permission in writing from the publisher.

Cover photo by Glenn Davis
www.secondflashphotography.com

www.codebreakeredu.com

This book is dedicated to the heretics, outliers, disruptors, and reluctant leaders that are bold enough to follow their passion!

I always write with my family in mind…
Dr. Kimberly, Franki Maria, and Danica Lyn

LEADER

The bright star that leads the way.

The sun that provides the world with light.

The rain that falls only in hopes of success and

growth,

Wishing to inflict

Pain and failure upon no one.

The rainbow that accepts all just the way they are,

The weeping willow that now stand tall,

The soft whisper of wind that blows until

movement has occurred,

That's you.

And you have made the world a better place.

Being the change, you want to see in the world.

Julie Lang

ACKNOWLEDGEMENTS

I acknowledge all educators in the world that make a difference every day no matter the circumstance.

What does it take to be you? What does it take to be great? What does it take to be a leader?

Expect a lot from yourself.
Believe in yourself.
Whatever it takes.

It's funny how your luck changes in a positive direction when you are committed to hard work. It becomes epic when your hard work is fun because you are engaged in your passion. A spark becomes a fire.

In addition to financial aid and scholarships, I worked my way through undergraduate school by performing magic and working in a magic shop at Fisherman's Wharf in San Francisco. Teaching was not my career choice upon graduation from the University of San Francisco. Believe it or not, after graduation, I was a magician and magic store entrepreneur until I found my pathway as an educator. I even performed on Donald Trump's yacht. Yes, that Donald Trump! Lots of stories there.

In the biggest event of my mystical career, I was chained up, handcuffed, nailed in a box, and thrown in a river (on purpose). When goal setting is commonplace, people understand the opportunities and self-

communicate the importance. I trained and practiced this feat for over a year. I made the decision to make it happen and it came to fruition on a newly erected riverfront in the town where I grew up.

It took research, physical fitness, escape training, magical practice, and coordination of resources. Even with all that preparation, things did not go as planned. But I made adjustments because of preparation.

Surround yourself with people that allow you to feel valued and happy. Create a place where everyone wants to be. That's the way we should approach every day. We have to. The minute we don't think we are making a difference, we aren't. We must connect that with one person that no one else can connect with. Start now and get connected to your inner and outer leadership. Don't live life like a rubric!

Thank you, Brian, Daphne, and all of the Code Breakers for believing in my disruption.

TABLE OF CONTENTS

FOREWORD

Dear Readers,

I have always imagined myself as a teacher. My heart never wavered from the call. I have known since kindergarten. So, it only made sense that I would read stacks of books on how to be that remarkable teacher. I read and read, and kept reading. Then I taught. I quickly discovered that books on teaching weren't always practical. If I wasn't careful, I would be overwhelmed with emotion because I couldn't recreate the experiences that methods books and inspirational stories expected of me. I have completed my first year of teaching, but still consider myself a new teacher. As I develop into a dedicated educator, I frequently return to Dr. Rudnesky's books and words of wisdom. They are authentic and refreshing.

As my middle school principal, Dr. Rudnesky was the first person to introduce me to the concept of true leadership. He always made it clear leadership wasn't about positional power but rather a choice. Simply put, you didn't have to be a star student or the captain of the sports team to lead. You just had to be the best version of YOU! This unique perspective of leadership is life giving for me as a teacher that copes with cerebral palsy. It allows me to see my worth. The way that Dr. Rudnesky defines leadership invites people to recognize that imperfections don't make someone less valuable.

Each day in my classroom, I strive to teach hope. I aim to articulate gratitude. I promise students often that we are achieving great things. I let students know that they are safe, but must make a decision to be brave. There is both a sense of risk and joy in encouraging students to be brave. It means that I openly admit that I am imperfect. I might misspell a word on the whiteboard. I might mispronounce a historical figure's name, or tell students that I'll research questions because I don't have all the answers. I didn't choose to teach for power or position. Teaching is an opportunity for me to demonstrate true leadership. I want students to see what it means to be passionately courageous. I teach through imperfection. I am completely myself in my classroom--- it amazes me daily!

Last week a student randomly gave me a sign that read, *"This classroom is My Happy Place."* It was a small and powerful gesture that helped me see that students might actually sense my commitment and happiness in helping them reach their promise. I couldn't teach with such a grateful spirit if Dr. Rudnesky did not share his sense of hope. It's fair to say that while I did not recreate a moment of hope, being in the classroom gives me a feeling of contentment---- Perhaps I am part of the reason someone has hope.

As you read, I challenge you to discover ways that you are impacting the world. Read as if you already know you're an inspiring leader. Let this be the read that restores your heart. Let Dr. Rudnesky's lessons be a reminder that you are a sense of hope for others.

Joyfully,

Julie
(Dr. R.'s former student and current teacher)

INTRODUCTION

What is the most powerful thing you can do?

LOVE

Start every day with love and gratitude. Watch what happens. If you feel my passion, you'll find yours. If I know your passion, I know how you learn. If you can learn, you can lead. If you can lead, you can start a movement. A movement changes your trajectory.

Everyone wants to live a life that matters. Living a *Fired Up* life with *Fired Up* Leadership sparks change that makes a difference! When your heart and soul are on fire, you become a "difference maker." There is no sky to your limit.

Your leadership journey is solidified in the 5th Domain - Passion. Some people are never excited about anything. I am on a mission to change that, and you will be, too!

I keep writing, preaching, and teaching about leadership for a number of reasons. One reason reflects the inability for people to have the opportunity to make the leap into the realm of change. If I can be that conduit to a better life, a purpose, or the right reason, then my leadership ability increases exponentially. Yours will, too. When one student looks in the mirror and sees themselves differently, a shift happens. A tipping point occurs. Not only do they see who they are but they see who they can become.

In order to generate understanding and attract nontraditional interest in leadership, *Fired Up* Leadership consists of five domains. These domains will give you a starting point to promote a positive climate and culture with leadership opportunities for everyone while balancing your life. Eliminate the myth that leadership is just for the popular students or for your administrative colleagues or for people with managerial titles.

LEADERSHIP IS A CHOICE

What your life becomes is entirely up to you. Never be afraid to fail and never be afraid to succeed either. You will have multiple failures that will lead to multiple successes. We are all in search of a life that matters. As you move towards fine-tuning the quality of your life, your goals and direction will move in line with your mission. Because you have the power of choice, some remarkable things can happen. Because you have the power of choice, some unremarkable things will happen, too. Every time you choose, you have an opportunity cost. This occurs when you relinquish an alternative to your choice. What did you give up? What can you gain?

Sometimes the future is now and we wait too long to choose. We may be reluctant or we may be under informed. Some decisions can be calculated, like where you go to college, or what you are wearing to a party. Some choices may be instantaneous like in an emergency or with an unexpected visit. Either way, we can be prepared to lead ourselves and the people around us.

This book will give you some insight and understanding of your ability to be a leader and the necessities for you to live a *Fired Up* life with *Fired Up* Leadership. Light the flame. Find a way to keep it lit. Pass the torch!

I received the following email from a student who had recently embarked on her college career.

"I just wanted to say thank you for being such an inspiration. Two days ago, I had an important scholarship interview. One of the most important components to get the competitive scholarship was Leadership. When they asked me what it means to be a leader, I knew the answer right away. To sum up what I said, I stated that being a leader is being a great influence & creating a change in my community. Today, I received the call and landed the scholarship! Without those opportunities, I don't know if I would've gotten it."

Let's get *Fired Up*, people! Stop right here and don't turn the page. Make a list of your barriers, fences, walls, barricades, blocks, and excuses to your happiness and the happiness of the people around you.

_____

_____

_____

_____

_____

_____

Did you list yourself as one of your barriers? Your happiness or unhappiness correlates directly with you and the decisions you make on a daily basis. When we work on ourselves first, we begin to move away from blaming others for the barriers we face. Whether it's your circumstances, your success, your education, your job, or the culture of your organization, start by looking in the mirror. How you see yourself now and, in the future, can make all the difference to your many successes and failures.

As human beings, we are imperfect and vulnerable. This will become who you are as a leader when you embrace the concept of continually making yourself better. *Fired Up Leadership* is not a moment. It's a movement.

You shouldn't be someone you are not. However, I also wholeheartedly believe that when we examine our imperfections, this provides an opportunity to eliminate our shortcomings and proceed in a positive direction that will teach us and the people around us to embrace our leadership capacity.

By creating more leaders, our inadequacies will be reduced both individually and as an organization. Our strengths help each other as we put together a powerful leadership team. As our strengths and opportunities increase synergistically, our weaknesses and threats are reduced significantly.

Jump in! Control what you can control. There is no new normal. There is no normal. Trust the people around you or build trust or get new people around you!

It is never too late to understand and accept your role as a leader but it is never too early, either. We need to value our future. We can make this happen by allowing people to have opportunities we did not have. Most importantly, you must first take care of yourself: Body, Mind, Heart, Spirit.

Before you lead that *Fired Up* life, you need a mindset. That mindset should be that you are not ordinary. Too many times we think of ourselves as not capable, and that outlook prohibits our success and our ability to accept our role as a leader.

BE EPIC NOT ORDINARY

THE NEW AGE OF HERETICS, OUTLIERS, AND DISRUPTORS

We are in the new era of heretics, outliers, and disruptors. We are preparing our students and children for jobs that will be outrageously uncommon. They will be shocking us in a good way because barriers are being lifted and expanded. Not very far in the future, even conventional and traditional careers will look nothing like they do now. They cannot. If they do, we are in trouble. The landscape is changing, and we need to fine-tune the process. We will adjust.

As I am writing, I am listening to the latest catastrophic school shooting and thinking about my daughters. My oldest is a senior at a university and my youngest, a high school junior. Their generation posts their feelings on social media because that is their norm. I saw that one daughter posted about her concern of gun control, and the other about her safety concerns for her family.

How do the heretics, a school shooting, and my children tie together? Maybe they don't in your world. In my universe, I want my daughters and every other student to be part of the thinking where we allow them to be creative. They must have opportunity to be imaginative and become great thinkers and difference makers. Our children and students need to know that we take their dreams and passions seriously. When they feel that we love them and believe in them, they will not only chase their dreams but they will become dream catchers.

We must also be vigilant but not afraid. No one should be worried about talking about creativity and "no box" thinking. No one should be terrified to attend school and go to work. These places should provide the opportunity to think, create, and invent. It may just have to look different.

Our children will be heretics because we need them to fly differently. We inspire them to shape their own paths where passion is a key to failures and successes. As they follow their path, they will find their voice. This will inspire others to find their passions and voices.

> # LOVE AND LEADERSHIP
> # CANNOT BE SEPARATED

Now that we are all thinking, let's start the conversation. We need to lead the wave of challenging opinions. Let's flip that model that doesn't allow everyone the same opportunities to think and express ideas. Let's stop saying we are proactive and be proactive. We are training our children to be accepting but we also need to make sure the line of communication and methods of communication are practiced and genuine. Let people know that you love them every day.

BE THE PERSON YOU WANT AROUND YOU

Sometimes we forget to be that person we need. A few months before I started to write this book, I received an invite to my fortieth, eighth-grade class reunion. I was immediately able to reply to the invitation and attach a picture of my eighth-grade class.

I show this picture when I talk to students and adults about leadership.

> # PEOPLE MAY NOT REMEMBER EXACTLY WHAT YOU DID OR WHAT YOU SAID, BUT THEY WILL ALWAYS REMEMBER HOW YOU MADE THEM FEEL.
>
> *Maya Angelou*

I display the picture to prove the truth in the statement. I cannot remember much about what I learned in eighth-grade but I can still name every student and tell you how each made me feel. I can tell you how every student made every other student feel, too.

People will always remember how you made them feel. That statement is true about your colleagues, friends, relatives, and coworkers. Long after you leave an organization, your legacy is defined by how you made people feel and how people made you feel. What do you want your legacy to be?

I ended up going to my eighth-grade reunion. I saw those same faces and those same smiles. I remembered those same feelings that I remember from eighth-grade. And we didn't talk about our eighth-grade curriculum once. It was great to see my old friends, and it was great to feel that happiness resonate from their smiles.

At the end of each year, I always had an individual meeting with all of the staffulty and students leaving our school. I asked each person how they felt. You never know another person's complete paradigm unless you know everything that person has gone through. I've always understood the importance and value of climate and culture in a school. If we are going to create a place where everyone wants to be through commitment, hard work, and leadership, then we must reflect on what stands in our way.

MOTIVATE YOURSELF INSPIRE OTHERS

Most people are worried about productivity rather than process. If you fine-tune the quality of the process, you'll create long-term productivity. How much time do you spend at work? Even if it's eight hours a day, that's half of your waking time. If you create a place where you want to be, I guarantee it will be a place where others want to be as well.

Leadership is not defined by a position or popularity. Leadership is a choice. I can debate this point with a number of contemporary leadership authors but you have to agree that everyone has a choice. You also have a choice as to the type of leader you portray. There are great leaders then there are great, bad leaders.

I call the great, bad leaders *Tater Tot Leaders*. Use the analogy of a school cafeteria. One kid throws a tater tot, and you have to admit, the size and shape are conducive to throwing. Then another kid throws one. Before you know it, the whole table is throwing tots. The one kid that threw the first tot is a leader, he has followers but he led in a bad direction. You can use the same comparison to some very bad world leaders that had whole countries following them.

Some researchers will debate that leaders are born. I would argue that there are some circumstances that may be advantageous to your quality of life and your opportunities because we aren't all born on a level playing field. However, as life progresses, your ability to lead and the direction you choose to lead are entirely up to you. In fact, this type (positional, disempowering) of leadership stifles the leadership potential within the organization.

These types of leaders lack the ability to reach their potential and sustain an organization's potential because they want to control everything and everyone. On the contrary, once you think you need invincibility you become a fairytale leader that will allow the organization to perish because you try to live forever without setting up your organization to thrive in the long-term.

Positional leaders that hoard control, stifle their colleagues wherever they go. These people define leadership as power, and they think there is a finite amount of leadership. These people will not promote leadership for everyone. Toxic leaders create "blind faith" that attracts followers but does not offer leadership opportunities for everyone. When expectations are lowered, so are outcomes.

All five domains of *Fired Up* Leadership are interconnected. Connecting and balancing all five will balance your  life and leadership. There will always be empty seats on the leadership bus. Climb on board. It's your choice and your destiny. The bus leaves every day. Be passionate about it or don't do it.

THE WOW! FACTOR

Leaders will emerge differently. Look for the *WOW!* Factor. You will know it when you see it. Feel it, own it. According to urbandictionary.com, the *WOW!* Factor is the distinctive appeal that an object, behavior or person has on others. An impressive display brought on by a certain object, behavior or person.

Let's imagine that you can work anywhere. Why did you choose to be there? Do you feel that WOW? When you talk to people about your organization, do they get that WOW? The *WOW!* Factor originates from a positive culture. What's the *WOW!* Factor that keeps people coming back each day?

You absolutely need the distinctive appeal that makes your organization different in a positive way. Some contemporary leadership literature documents that you do not need enthusiasm to be an effective leader. I disagree. I see enthusiasm carry over to all aspects of an organization. Positive leadership generates enthusiasm.

Most of my professional career has been devoted to education and leadership. You may think some of the examples I use won't work in your organization. Keep an open mind. These examples will work in any organization. Our school had visitors from all over the world. From as far away as Japan, people examined our climate, culture, and technology influence. One of the common themes was happiness. One visitor stated that the first thing she noticed was smiles. It was a *WOW!* Factor for her.

Another shared theme is kindness. Granted, none of us are perfect at it, but practice kindness on a daily basis. Kindness is not a one-time event or a moment. A day or week of kindness isn't enough. It should be part of your daily repertoire. It is a movement.

Even though excitement permeated from the individuals walking down the hallways, our walls actually inspired visitors. One of my goals was not to have any blank walls. As soon as you walked in the front door, you got that *WOW!* Factor. From a multi-colored banner that spells LEADERSHIP to the compelling artistic tiles with legacy words of acceptance or the intriguing quilts hanging from the ceiling, you could not help but ask, "What is going on?"

When you are in a leadership school, you know it right away. It is not a question you ask. You see the way people treat you, and the way they act. The principal gets treated the same as a lunch server. Likewise, every member of the organization treats you a certain way. They make you feel important because you are important. Likewise, you make them feel important.

The following is an excerpt from a letter sent by a student during our last week of school. She understands the power of abundance mentality as it applies to love and leadership.

I have more respect for the unsung heroes of our educational system. Like custodial staff, secretaries, and lunch room personnel. With this, you have shown us that much is the same in life and no one is any more or less important than anyone else. Everyone in our school practiced this and students were allowed to possess an inner light, and no one tried to stop the glow......School was so much a part of our lives, not only because we spent so much time there but because we enjoyed the time we spent. It's hard to get used to pep rallies that promote just sports instead of academic achievement, character, and leadership. I see now, while experiencing the diverse environment of high school, why you have to keep refining the one thing you can change - yourself...In closing, I love the quote, 'Can you hear with your heart?' because I truly believe that you can lead people to truth by love. Thanks for an awesome four years - the memories, the fun times, and most of all the character altering teachings on being a positive leader now and forever.

WOW! That got me *Fired Up*! I have to keep reminding myself that it was written by a fourteen-year-old. It just blows my mind and shows me the realization of what anyone is capable of accomplishing when you open up that leadership door.

LEADERSHIP STYLES

Fired Up Leadership is based on two different leadership styles; Transformational Leadership and Servant Leadership.

Transformational leaders focus on the people in the organization and inspire them to reach their potential while creating leadership opportunities for everyone. Where transformational leadership is promoted, people are challenged to reach their full potential by aligning them with tasks that are meaningful. Meaningless tasks do not engage people over time. People begin to feel unimportant. People naturally want to make a positive difference. These positive outcomes start from within. Positivity is spread just as easily as negativity.

Servant leadership is similar to transformational leadership because your organizational success depends on the attention you devote to your colleagues. The highest point occurs in creating as many leaders as possible. The more leaders you create, the more successful your organization will become. A synergistic effect allows barriers to be eradicated.

> # CREATE A PLACE WHERE EVERYONE WANTS TO BE AND GREAT RESULTS CAN BE ACHIEVED

In his book *The Servant,* James C. Hunter describes the need to serve before you can lead. This theory dates back thousands of years. Without love there is no leadership.

A compliment to servant leadership and transformational leadership is resultant leadership. When you connect a positive climate and culture to your workplace, you get positive results.

In the Dalai Lama and Howard Cutler's book, *The Art of Happiness,* the authors discover that unhappy people are more self-centered. Happy people are generally more sociable, flexible, and accepting. It is almost common sense. Resultant leaders are always creating opportunities for more people to become leaders. It creates synergy and "pays forward" chances for a positive culture.

Many people synonymously define leadership as a position. However, positional leadership is based on a "position." Manager, CEO, principal, boss, and supervisor are just job designations. A title does not necessarily translate to positive leadership although many great leaders hold positions of authority. The truly great leaders in "positions of authority" continually gather information and proceed in a positive direction based on stakeholders' and consumers' success.

These positions are greatly enhanced through the other styles of leadership that were mentioned. An inspirational leader continually pursues the creation of more leaders rather than more followers. A negative "positional" leader tries to define leadership by the need to be "in charge."

Great leaders are not afraid to get their hands dirty. *Fired Up* Leadership needs all stakeholders in an organization to move smoothly towards a common destination. Self-serving leadership only creates a toxic environment.

Through research, experience, and mutual themes, the *Fired Up* process is divided into five areas, or domains, that will balance your opportunities.

1. Self-Management/Organization
2. Communication/Listening
3. Critical Thinking, Problem Solving and Team Building
4. Character and Service
5. Passion

These concepts have been taught to middle school, high school, college students and adults of all ages. *Fired Up* Leadership provides timeless principles that have common threads for all of us.

THE FIRST DOMAIN

SELF-MANAGEMENT AND ORGANIZATION

The single most important factor that will contribute to your leadership style is YOU. Your experiences have given you a view of the world. Before you can change anything, start with yourself. Dig deeply into your body, mind, heart, and spirit. Balance in the "whole person" approach is your biggest ally. This is also an excellent tactic for teaching. Because you understand self-care, you become more effective at teaching to the whole child and the whole person.

You must comprehend what you already know to begin your leadership journey. Never forget where you came from or you will not know where you are going. Use a constructivist approach to maximize your ability to lead. Use other people's paradigms along with your own to interpret a better reality. Transformational and servant leadership will transcend your results in life and leadership.

Our brains are wired to favor familiarity. We are bias towards environments that are unfamiliar. We all have implicit bias. That is one reason that we need to bring leadership opportunities to everyone. When we do, our chances for leadership success are increased.

You may not remember everything that happened to you when you were a five-year-old but you definitely have memories of some things that have shaped you. Those positive feelings from your memories will allow you to build a better you and a healthier future. As odd as it may sound, the pain and the glory will stay with you.

Even though many of us may have been assigned positions of leadership as young adolescents or teenagers, we never really understood leadership until we became adults. Then we made the necessary connections. If you are a pre-adult, adolescent, or young adolescent reading this book, take note. Most everyone associates leadership with a position or title. Your title, your position does not qualify a person as a leader.

Cura Personalis is a Latin phrase and a Jesuit concept that translates to "Care for the entire person." I heard the phrase for the first time from my oldest daughter, Franki Maria. She attended Saint Joseph's University in Philadelphia, a Jesuit school. Her assignment for the university newspaper was to find and interview someone from SJU that witnessed the Pope's visit to Philadelphia twice, once in 1978 and again in 2015. She discovered the oldest Jesuit priest on campus, Father James W. Moore. During the interview, he proudly told Franki Maria, "If you write anything about me, please write about my commitment to *Cura Personalis.*" He was committed to the whole student, the whole person. He was not focused partially on a domain or a test score or a moment in the academic career of a young adult. Fr. Moore cared about growth in all areas of a person that could eliminate barriers to success and allow people to examine their full potential. He went above and beyond the curriculum because it made sense. That is what all great educators do. I applaud Fr. Moore for his commitment to people. I am grateful to my daughter for bringing this parallel concept of the whole person into my world.

If you are trying to lose weight, the worst thing you can do is go on a diet. Becoming healthier needs to be a lifestyle. Your eating habits need to contribute to your exercise and your mental health along with your spirit. When you are balanced, your potential is within your grasp. Your path leads you to your EPIC. Where your Exceptional talents meet your Passion guided by your Intelligence and Character, therein lies your EPIC.

MANAGE THINGS LEAD PEOPLE

When I look at the job pool, I avoid people that lack self-management. After you hire someone, offer tools for success through a variety of professional development. Instead of training managers, we need to train leaders. Part of any job training needs to be self-management as a prelude to leadership. The lack of self-management can be the ruination of a new career, a new semester, a new project. It takes continual fine-tuning. Start with goal-setting.

GOALS

When we start organizing our lives, we must begin with goals. In the broadest form of a statement, I feel that any time we want to do something; we should do it, accomplish it. We will have many failures in addition to our many successes. Remarkable things can be achieved when we eliminate common barriers of insignificance, time management, and lack of commitment.

By that statement, I mean: Look in the mirror to see not only who you are but who you can become. That's when the tipping point occurs. Believe in yourself. Keep self-communicating.

One of the biggest forms of identity theft is telling someone they cannot accomplish something. Keep dreaming so big that it freaks people out! Your dreams develop into goals, and when you write them down your chances of success increase considerably. Goal setting is remarkably powerful. Try it! I write my daily and weekly goals down as soon as I sit at my desk. I write my yearly goals on something obnoxious and put that on my desk. I'm currently looking at a beach ball!

Of course, you need a plan to achieve a goal. I saw a remarkable plan when I observed a seventh-grade language arts class. The teacher implemented different methods of formative assessment. Each student kept a formative assessment log and wrote in their progress each day for each goal. In this case, a learning objective. Set your goal, deliver your plan, and chart your progress. Change your plan or method of achievement if you are not mastering the goal or objective. Repeat.

The following is an excerpt from an essay by a former high school student. Her dream was to become an Emergency Medical Technician. She wrote down her goal and implemented a plan. Guess what? She is now enjoying a career as an EMT. She loves what she does. Did you catch that? It is her passion.

One of Dr. R.'s biggest motivators was telling us all to raise the bar. 'Expect a lot from yourself or no one else will.' Being the best we could be was in a way expected throughout middle school, although still a choice. If we choose to do the bare minimum then that was your decision, but if we decided to exceed each and every self-accomplishment then we showed ourselves that hard work really does pay off. I saw it with my own eyes after I accomplished personal goals, from something as simple as studying for an English test, to things at greater levels such as winning second place at the science fair, or graduating middle school. Keeping that in the back of my mind has brought me far and will continue to take me to better places. Most people can't say their principal inspired them to do much more than stay out of their office. I consider myself fortunate to have been introduced to Dr. R. There are countless lessons that I've learned from him and that I know my peers have also taken away as well. I've learned to be a better person through his encouragement and strive to be all that I can be. Like he always said, 'Work hard, be successful, have fun!', and because of him, I always will."It was not because of me that she achieved her goal. It was because of her introduction to herself as a leader and her ability to follow her passion that allowed her to become a real "difference maker."

On the first day of our new school year, I always asked everyone in our school to write their goals down along with me. What they wrote them on depended on our yearly school theme. One year, we had gold bricks *(There's No Place Like Home)* and another year we had sea shells *(Belhaven Beach)*. I coached my daughter's softball team and asked the girls to write them on a softball and keep the ball in their gloves so they have to look at them every time we practiced. At our yearly leadership camp for students and their parents we had students reflect on their goals for the new school year and write them on magnets. The magnets were hung on the inside of their lockers.

Goal setting becomes a mindset. Success becomes a mindset. A plan of action must go into effect after you write down your goal. That's where some people get lost. What do you need to do to accomplish your goal? This could take training, professional development, or coaching but any worthwhile goal will take a commitment. Your commitment might be as simple as creating a time to do homework or spending a night watching a movie with your family. It might be hard like changing your mindset or getting an advanced college degree.

THE MOST IMPORTANT COMPONENT OF GOAL SETTING IS TO GET STARTED

Whatever the level of difficulty, your goal needs self-communication. Tell yourself what you are going to achieve: I will walk two miles. I will stop eating so much sugar. I will read twenty minutes a day. I will make my bed before I leave the house. I will practice mindfulness. I will talk to my parents. I will talk to my children. I will be a better listener. When you keep those promises to yourself, larger goals become real and attainable.

How you define success or happiness may be different than another person's view of life. My paradigm is sometimes positioned on the number of smiles I see on the people around me. Count the smiles the next time you enter a room with people. Sometimes it's just that simple.

This is a friend's plan after writing down her goals:

Here is my plan for what looks like a very busy year...when I wake up in the morning, before my feet hit the floor, I plan on thinking of three things that I am thankful for and three things I want to get accomplished on that day...just three. I obviously am thankful for so much more and plan on doing so much more. But if I can just take that one minute to gain clarity and perspective, I think I will be able to tackle just about anything with a smile on my face and joy enough to share!

So, on day one, I stuck to my plan. However, I was still feeling just slightly overwhelmed at the enormity of a new school year. And then a friend sent me a silly message that literally made me laugh out loud. I still have that smile on my face as an exclamation point on the love of friends and family that fills my days and nights. With that care, with that support that we all have if we look for it, every challenge becomes just another hurdle...some are the low ones, some are the high ones that will trip us at times. But there are always people who will be there to lift us up and take us forward. On this day, I am very grateful for all of them, for all of you.

TIME

What are you going to do with it? Most of your life is planned for you until you graduate from high school. Up until high school, you know what time you arrive, leave, practice, meet, and eat. When you hit college or the "real world", time management becomes a real thing. Time becomes essential in achieving long term success.

The pandemic of 2020 threw people off of their schedule. We had a renewed experience with planning. Did you schedule your important tasks and the fun experiences you needed? That period should have sparked organization.

My brief summation consists of this: schedule the things you want to do around the things you have to do. You know when you work, sleep, practice, have mandatory meetings, etc. Schedule your exercise, meal preparation, mindfulness, yoga, art, family time, and whatever is most important to you. We schedule dentist appointments, so why not schedule our workouts too?

> # 86,400 · 1,440 · 24 · 1
> ## SECONDS · MINUTES · HOURS · DAY
> ## DID YOU GET EVERYTHING
> ## ACCOMPLISHED TODAY?

Probably not but the day isn't over. These are non-renewable resources. If you wrote down your goals, your chances of success just increased. With this much time to work around, no matter how busy you think you are, YOU can make a real difference.

COMMITMENT

A friend of mine, Dr. Larry Biddle, always demonstrates three levels of commitment when he speaks to an audience about leadership:

> Level One: Try
> Level Two: Do my best.
> Level Three: Whatever it takes

Think about this for a second: Have you ever flown on a plane? The pilot gets on the intercom, "Hi, I'm Pilot Bob. I'm going to try to get to your destination." I have actually been on a flight where the pilot told us, "We are experiencing heavy turbulence, I am going to do my best to land us safely." Sorry, Bob, I want the pilot that's actually going to get me to my destination. Or what if your heart doctor told you they were going to try and cure you? No! I want the doctor that can actually cure me.

The third level of commitment reminds of a Star Wars movie. In *The Empire Strikes Back,* Luke Skywalker trains with Master Yoda on planet Dagobah. Luke, through his newly discovered Jedi powers, is *trying* to raise his X-Wing Starfighter out of the misty, murky swamp. The ship starts to rise when suddenly Luke gives up. He says, "I can't." Yoda replies with one of my favorite quotes, "No! Try not. Do or do not, there is no try."

We painted that quote on the wall in our building. It reminded us every day of that third level of commitment. I secretly want to be a Jedi master but I have not been able to purchase an authentic lightsaber. I still partake in Jedi mind tricks once in a while but not in any official capacity.

The quote on our wall has a picture of Yoda next to it. The students that painted the mural had left Yoda's head as an outline. Another student had asked if he could paint the head green. Heck yes! The mural is located in a stairwell the upper-class students used every day. I have no idea how he accessed the school or where he got the paint but Yoda's head was painted green the next day. I saw the student turned painter, John, proudly watching all the other students admiring the newly updated painting. *WOW!* Factor. John is connected to the school forever. He is an intelligent, yet underachieved student. That moment changed him. He became a different person. That one act allowed him to become a leader. He felt it, and so did his teachers.

When we self-communicate the concept of commitment through hard work and preparation, we change our mindset. We stop making excuses and begin to find a way to make things happen, in a positive way.

There will always be self-centered, hidden agendas from people trying to build followers.

When our goal is to create more leaders, the focus moves away from useless meetings, bureaucracy, and meaningless data. Find your passion. Self-communicate your goals and change your environment in a positive way.

In addition to self-communication, self-reflection becomes a part of fine-tuning the quality of your life. In the foyer of our building, we hung a sign the length of the 20 foot wall. I was facilitating a breakout session at a leadership conference, and I asked the audience of adults if they noticed the sign. Everyone had to pass by it on the way in. Not one person remembered the sign. The sign reads: LEADERSHIP. Conversely, I facilitated the same session to students a few hours later and asked the same question. Almost all of the students noticed the sign. Why?

As adults, we are already making our next move or talking without listening or not stopping to enjoy the moment. Carpe Momentum! Seize the

Moment. Stop and reflect. Are you where you want to be? I hope so. If not, leave or change your environment. Create more leaders instead of looking for more followers. It works. If you don't believe me, ask a student. LEADERSHIP: it's on a wall near you. Put it up and seize the moment! Self-communicate. Our future depends on it.

ViSiON AND MiSSiON

Every organization should have a vision and a mission displayed prominently. Ours, "We inspire life-long learners and leaders" was painted in our foyer, twenty feet high. As a prelude to your organization having a mission, you must also have one. Mine is, "Continually fine-tune the quality of my life and the lives of the people around me through commitment and hard work while having fun." It started out much longer but as I got older, I realized this is what I was doing. I want it to be my legacy.

> **POTENTiAL MiNUS COMMiTMENT EQUALS NOTHiNG**

If you haven't already, create your personal mission statement. Your mission should be in line with your goals. There's a spot in the back of this book. You can always whittle it down. Who are you and what do you want to bring to the people around you?

A great leader has passion for the organization's vision and mission.

What do you consider the essential qualities of a leader? Go ahead, think about it and write it down. I polled over 10,000 students over the last ten years. What I discovered is that young people recognize the importance of integrity. By far, the number one answer was integrity and positive character traits. Without positive character, there is no positive leadership.

Each year our school had a leadership camp for incoming eighth-grade students. The school houses fifth through eighth grades. This solidified what I already knew, leadership is possible at any age. We set the tone for their final year in our school by kicking it off with a day's worth of training. This is the beginning of the end in a chapter of their lives. We also invite parents. Those that attended saw what we wanted to accomplish. We were able to connect multiple stakeholder groups.

The day begins with food and music, both safe bets. People like to eat and people like to listen to music. Most of the theory we use was grounded in servant and transformational leadership; however, the underlying themes were collegiality, team-building, and problem-solving. We began with self-management and organization. These are all essential components of long-term, successful leadership. After light snacks, we delve into some review of concepts, then a team-building activity: Name "one great thing" about your school. This is something fast and easy that brings out pride. Our new theme and service-learning platform for the year are introduced and discussed. As mentioned earlier, goals are a big part of the upcoming "new year."

A GOAL WITH NO PLAN IS NO GOAL AT ALL

Towards the end of the day, we have the campers describe one thing they want to see their school do in the near future. It has to be something they see as attainable, and it has to be something they can follow through with. We have them write it on big poster paper and tape it to the wall. The day is finished by debriefing with the students and reinforcing what we accomplished. The real work, I tell them, starts when they leave. One of the most important components is that stakeholders are given a voice. As a leader in your school, you must follow-through with some of their ideas because it matters. Consider everything.

ATTITUDE

You have total control over two things every day: yourself and your attitude. It starts as soon as you get out of bed. When your feet hit the floor, you've already overcome one obstacle. Then when you turn on the light in your bathroom, don't scream. That reflection in the mirror is you! Some people let the slightest thing set them off in a negative direction. Who are you going to be today? Choose your attitude; make it a positive one! Your attitude may control your destiny. Your attitude will definitely control your leadership. See every barrier and conflict as an opportunity to improve the quality of your leadership ability. It's not always easy but it will allow you and the people around you to be more successful in the long-term.

People that are negative, underachievers, and complainers become toxic after a while. It is much easier to complain than to do something to improve. It's easier to sit on the couch and eat chips and drink soda than to exercise and eat right. It's much easier to bash your colleagues than to take charge of yourself and your attitude. It's much easier to complain than to join the positive revolution. Instead of a complaint, praise a coworker. Instead of underachieving, reach your potential through commitment and hard work. Instead of bashing your colleagues, get *Fired Up*! Fuel your fire!

A POSITIVE ATTITUDE MAKES QUANTUM LEAPS IN YOUR ABILITY TO DO ANYTHING

Every Monday, after I wrote my goals for the day and the week, I sent an email to all the staffulty (staff and faculty) called "Tip of the Week." I often wondered if anyone read them. This is a response from a teacher that not only read them but used the tips with her students and her family. It is a great connection to the 1st Domain.

For this week's tip of the week I spent some time asking students how they will make a difference. Responses ranged from taking out the trash for their parents, telling someone 'I love you', to helping a friend. I'm a teacher, mother, and wife. I spend most of my time taking care of others first and thinking of myself last. On the way home Monday, I was thinking about how I was going to do something different for my sons to make a difference. After I picked up my kids from school, we rushed home to grab a snack and immediately left for their drum lessons, and I had to stop to get coffee if I was going last till 9pm. As I was getting coffee, a police officer offered to pay (the situation reminded me of a story you told at a staffulty meeting a couple of years ago). I started to think about the tip of the week again and how the little things people do to make a difference can add up to big things that can change the world. You make a difference every day because it has become a part of who you are, not a task to check off your list. You truly inspire me to make a difference in the lives of the people I interact with every day. I want 'making a difference' to be part of who I am and not a task to check off. I am working on it...I wanted to share this with you because I never seem to have the time to tell people that I appreciate what they do. Sometimes people leave and you never tell them how much their positivity changed your outlook as a teacher. I don't want to let more days pass without ever telling the people around me how much I have become a better teacher, mother, and wife because of them. Thank you.

GRATITUDE BREEDS GRATITUDE

SUMMARY

Take out your phone. Go to the calendar app. Set an event for one year from today. Write in the event: Am I where I want to be? Let's see what happens.

Your chances of success increase significantly when you have goals, you write them down, and you have a plan. There is no secret to success; it takes hard work and commitment. Your attitude is a significant factor to your success. Don't ever let anyone tell you that you cannot accomplish something.

Many of our limitations are self-inflicted. Spend time creating a personal mission statement. What do you want your legacy to be? Concentrate on leadership styles that are in line with your vision and mission. Your leadership style should enable you to spend time with the people within your organization. Your strengths should eliminate the weaknesses of others in your organization. Likewise, the strengths of others in your organization should eliminate your weaknesses.

Stay balanced in all areas: body, mind, heart, spirit. Encourage other people to stay balanced. What is your EPIC? Find it! If you are an educator, always use the whole child model. Be able to step out of your comfort zone and expand it.

Take the following survey. If you score less than three in any area, target that specific area for improvement. Your total score serves as a benchmark.

THE 1ST DOMAIN SURVEY
SELF - MANAGEMENT AND ORGANIZATION

1=Never 2=Sometimes 3=Frequently 4=Always

I set goals by writing them down
1   2   3   4

I have a plan to achieve my goals
1   2   3   4

I am organized
1   2   3   4

I am polite
1   2   3   4

I set a positive example for others
1   2   3   4

I continually build my leadership legacy

1   2   3   4

My workplace/school offers leadership opportunities

1   2   3   4

THE SECOND DOMAIN

COMMUNICATION AND LISTENING

ruce Springsteen, the iconic American singer-songwriter, summed up why leadership became one of my passions when he said, "It comes down to trying to make people happy, less lonely, but also being a conduit for a dialogue about the events of the day, the issues that impact people's lives, personal and social and political and religious. That's how I always saw the job of our band. That was my service." Creating more leaders is my service. If I can bridge that gap and open minds for people to see themselves differently, the positivity will shut down the naysayers, disrupt the status quo, and then get rid of it. One of the keys to making this happen is communication. Self-communicate who you are becoming on your leadership journey. Before you can give service, you have to make yourself happy. In other words, give service to yourself before you give it to someone else. Service through communication is one component we can all bring to the rest of the world once we decide to live that *Fired Up* life.

Once you commit, it's a constant ride to improve yourself and the people around you. Ask some people why they aren't successful, and they will blame everyone but themselves. There comes a time in your life when you need to take control, find your voice, and allow other people opportunities that you didn't have at their age. For me, opportunity spans many different roles, and it will for you, too.

BECOME A GREAT LISTENER

We communicate many different ways, both verbally and nonverbally: read, write, talk, listen, and body language. Listening will truly become your biggest relationship builder as a leader. In Stephen R. Covey's book, The 7 Habits of Highly Effective People, he lists five levels of listening to truly become an empathic listener. They include ignoring, pretend listening, selective listening, attentive listening, and empathic listening.

Most people want to talk more than they want to listen. Even quiet people are not great listeners. Even your closest friends are not stellar listeners, and by nature they don't want to listen. People will interpret their conversation with you as what they want to hear. They will interpret your conversation with how they relate to the topic. Most people interpret a conversation selectively. They sometimes hear what they want to hear, not what you are actually saying. Some are so anxious to speak, they do not listen. Remember, perception is reality.

To become a great listener we must practice. It's like any other area in our lives where we choose to go beyond proficiency. Practice listening to other people and actually try to interpret what they are saying. If you do not fully understand, ask. Some of the worst listening techniques are cutting people off, raising your voice, and really not knowing how the person feels. Great listening does not come easy but when you achieve it, you will know and so will the other person. Listen to people with knowledge you do not yet possess.

These situations will push you to make quantum leaps in your success if you learn to listen to them. Remember, listening does not mean agreeing. Treat everyone as if they are special because they are special. This concept can make or break any relationship. Unconditional communication - it's called listening.

> ## PAY ATTENTION TO PEOPLE THAT VIEW SITUATIONS WITH A DIFFERENT PARADIGM THAN YOURS

We have had the privilege to hire former students on more than one occasion. Even though this person was in a temporary position, her efforts and performance were exemplary. She was able to view our vision from different paradigms.

I cannot thank you enough for giving me the opportunity to begin my teaching career at Belhaven Middle School. It has been such a wonderful four 4 months. From day 1, I felt like a part of the Belhaven family. There was not a day that I did not wake up excited to come to work. I am truly inspired by the spirit, positive energy, creativity, sense of humor, collaborative nature, and passion for teaching that I have seen in the staffulty. I am inspired by teachers who continuously strive to be better by setting new goals, taking risks, and never being satisfied. And, of course, I am inspired by the process that opens up leadership for everyone, which continues to blow me away! Even in this short time. I have grown so much as a teacher and as a person. Belhaven will always hold a very special place in my heart. Thank you for everything.

SELF - COMMUNICATION

In the simplest form, self-communication is communicating with yourself. When we say it out loud, it may feel silly, but we really need to tell ourselves what we are capable of accomplishing. No matter what our barriers, there is no ceiling on our achievements. Don't ever sell yourself short. If you think you can, then you can. Expect a lot from yourself or no one else will. High expectations are catchy. You must first communicate this to yourself before you can pass on the theory to other people in your organization. Your self-communication becomes part of your daily communication to the people around you.

One example that keeps creeping up in my life, and maybe yours, is cancer . It seems like there are more people you know that have been touched by cancer than not. I'll share a personal story about my wife although it would be easy to share several other stories of people that I know or you know because this disease is so commonplace.

THERE IS A REMARKABLE DIFFERENCE BETWEEN A COMMITMENT OF 99 AND 100

Vic Conant

When you put your mind to it, your positive thoughts can allow your body to overcome many barriers. These accomplishments may take hard work and commitment but it all starts with a positive mindset and confidence in yourself. Again, it all starts with YOU. You must self-communicate a positive message before you expect to communicate an optimistic future to anyone else.

Let's get back to my wife, Kim. She has three college degrees including a doctorate of educational leadership. Kim knows the words to every song written in the 1980s. In other words, she is a lot of fun. My wife is a wonderful role model for our daughters as well as many other strong women.

A few years before she was diagnosed with breast cancer, her sister also fought a courageous battle with cancer. As could be expected, my wife was devastated when her sister passed away. Now, she had her own battle to prepare and fight. Make no mistake, my wife is a warrior. She is also the type of person that will scream bloody murder if she sees a spider in the house and call a neighbor to come remove it if I'm not home.

Her first reaction to the news of her cancer was met with total depression. Her sister's passing magnified her bout. All of her friends and family kept pumping her up with positive communication. She didn't bond to her own inner strength until she had a chance meeting with her hairdresser who connected her to a book by Ernest Holmes about the power of positive thinking. That book reinforced what Kim already knew she could accomplish. She made a commitment to positivity and self-communicated that message constantly.

Ernest Holmes is the author of *The Science of Mind* and many other metaphysical books. His books echo a familiar theme that can be found in other books like *Think and Grow Rich* by Napoleon Hill. This book also resonates the positive power of what I now call "self-communication."

Part of her proactive approach to attacking this disease was to balance all aspects of her life. It was an opportunity to self-communicate that her life was calling. How was she going to answer? She answered by becoming a healthier person in general. She knew it was necessary to make the social, emotional, physical, and mental aspects of herself achieve equal levels of health. So that's what she did. Her surgeries were approached with new meaning. I would like to say they went smoothly but there were obstacles. Every setback was assembled with some type of success and positive attitude. The next year was greeted with a new outlook. She fed her appetite with positive thoughts throughout every phase of her life. Although fatigued during many occasions, she rarely took a day off from her job as an educator. My wife, Kim, was an example for everyone, most importantly for herself, of the power of positive thinking and self-communicating that.

She anxiously crossed the days off the calendar as she advanced through her chemotherapy and radiation treatments. Our family wrote a list on the wall of our closet in permanent marker of things we wanted to do when her treatments were complete. As she lost her hair, she wore her different wigs with fashionable honor. Except for her inner circles, most people did not know she was going through treatment. Most importantly, she always communicated a positive vibe to herself and the people around her.

We all have met people that have approached life as my wife did. Then there are people who have condemned themselves to failure of everything with negligible barriers. These people play the blame game instead of taking control. They never reach their potential because there is no commitment. Your life is special. What are you going to do with it? You must first self-communicate your value before you can communicate with anyone else. Self-communication creates confidence and power.

Self-communication is a vital part of goal setting. If you have a long-term goal, self-communication must be a continual part of your plan to achieve your goal. Positive self-talk is a component of self-worth. Instead of, "I can't, I can't, I can't," make it, "I can, I can, I can." This will turn into "we can, we can, we can." What ifs turn into I ams.

If you are a parent or a teacher, think back to the times when one of your kids just wouldn't stop talking. You may have been frustrated to a point where you told them to be quiet. I try to cherish the times now when my kids won't keep quiet. They just want someone to listen. If you are a teacher, the most valuable gift you get this year may be sitting in the front row of your classroom.

> **YOU CAN BE THAT ONE PERSON TO CONNECT WITH AND INSPIRE THAT ONE STUDENT OR COLLEAGUE THAT NO ONE ELSE CAN SEEM TO UNDERSTAND**

I guarantee this; students will always remember how you made them feel. I can remember every teenager in my eighth-grade class and how every kid made me and every other person feel. Likewise, I can remember how every teacher and colleague made me feel over the years. You remember those emotions, too.

Communication happens in your life all day, all the time, and it comes in many forms both verbal and non-verbal. You need to continually fine-tune the communication process, especially listening. What message are you sending your family, friends, and colleagues? You must communicate outwardly the same positive outlook that you self-communicate. Sometimes, we need to be nicer to the people closest to us.

YOU BECOME WHAT YOU THINK ABOUT NEGATIVE THOUGHTS REAP NEGATIVE RESULTS IF YOU THINK POSITIVE THOUGHTS YOU WILL GET POSITIVE RESULTS

Earl Nightingale

Here is another example of self-communication and goal setting from a former student.

It was wonderful to see you all on Tuesday. I am still in awe about how much I am remembered and appreciated. It makes my heart melt. It is a privilege to return to such a warm welcome. Belhaven (School) is an extremely special community! As I walked through our hallways, I was overwhelmed with a fresh sense of determination and positive energy. To use Dr. R's words, I was fired up! Within minutes of being in our school I was reminded of where my desire for learning and positive leadership developed. You all have made a difference in my life that is unforgettable. Thank you is an understatement for what my support system at Belhaven School has done for me.

During my visit I told Dr. R about how important the Queens University Motto has become for me as a student but more as an individual. After giving it tremendous thought, I realized our motto, 'Non ministrari, sed ministrare' - Not to be served, but to serve - really means living leadership out loud. (It is also what you do each day as teachers). Thanks so much for your passion! Thank you for inviting me to speak to you all on Tuesday. You all were super respectful and great listeners. Give yourselves a power clap. You made my day worth five stars! Dream big and smile wide! Best wishes in accomplishing your goals.

TECHNOLOGY AND COMMUNICATION

The possibilities that technology brings to communication absolutely thrills and scares me at the same time. I am privileged to be an educator for over thirty years, and I am privileged to have two beautiful, wonderful daughters. Their communication includes the backdrop the world provides. Communication through technology happens so fast, and it goes viral quickly which makes it both advantageous and a threat at home and at work.

According to a recent Gallup poll, the most popular form of communication for people under fifty is texting. Smart phones quickly took over the information overload. In Covey's book, *The 8th Habit,* listening still holds the highest frequency in face-to-face communication.

One main factor to infuse in tech communication is positive character traits. Among other components to technology, the etiquette is to think before you act. Many people feel masked by social media to the point of anonymity. We must self-communicate the importance of integrity with social media and allow our modeling to pave the positive way for our students and colleagues.

PUBLIC SPEAKING

Another important component of communication in *Fired Up Leadership* is public speaking. In some instances, technology can stifle public speaking. Look at the end of any teenager's hand. You'll see some type of gadget attached. While my daughter was in middle school, she had friends we never even saw because of text messaging (not necessarily a bad thing but it didn't promote the public speaking component and it stifled socialization).

As leaders, we must create these public speaking opportunities. These chances can occur in a variety of settings, mostly by **doing it**. In a school, you can build it into any curriculum. In a corporation you can build public speaking into meetings with presentations, research, and practice. Because people may not create these opportunities on their own, we must lead them to these opportunities so that they may become habits. We must lead by example.

Glossophobia is the fear of public speaking. Ask anyone to list some of their fears and someone almost always says public speaking. As a matter of fact, when I searched the topic, the fear of speaking was listed before the fear of death. That's right, most people would rather die than get in front of people and speak. According to a 2013 *Forbes* magazine article, the fear of speaking is usually connected to some other fear. It makes sense because when I researched professional development in our organization, one fear was speaking and/or teaching in front of colleagues. Even people that were exemplary teachers feared getting in front of their colleagues to teach or present.

Any organization can flourish or be destroyed by external and/or internal communication. For instance, consider where the pockets of negative and positive communication are in your organization. Try to attack the negative through honesty. Be prepared however as not everyone is ready to hear honesty if it's not their perception. Negaholics will waste their time complaining rather than doing something in a positive manner. They are in the way of your leadership as well as theirs. *Perception is reality.* Make the real reality the real perception. Some people have a preconceived notion of leadership. In a school, if any stakeholder does not feel they can lead then they will not. When I hired a new teacher, aide, secretary, custodian, they needed to know that as soon as they crossed that threshold, they had to accept their role as a leader. They were no more or less important than anyone else in the organization.

Educators misinterpret leadership just like anyone else in any organization. They think a position and title solidifies leadership. "Only administrators are leaders" is a common misconception. Position is just that, a position. Leadership is a choice and people must feel comfortable making that choice. They must feel supported. They have to feel empowered.

Here is an example that I experienced in our school. We changed the perception by changing the culture. Administrators cannot be the only leaders. A leadership school becomes a school of excellence when people are given opportunities without isolation or fear of retribution. The creation of leaders and leadership opportunities become exponential because people create them for each other. No one wants to be left behind.

The following email is from a teacher that became *Fired Up* with the creation of a different culture that allowed her to see herself differently.

I am a teacher of twenty-five years. I reached a low point in my career about ten years ago when my curriculum was eliminated. I felt unappreciated and the life contributions I taught to the students were unimportant. Unfortunately, I internalized those feelings and started to believe I was unimportant, and I had nothing to offer the profession I dearly loved. I was ready to leave my career prematurely.

Why did I stay? What keeps me inspired and connected to the world of teaching, learning, and leadership? Fortunately for my coworkers and me, we had the opportunity to become leaders in our own right.

This history is important to the story because our school's climate and culture is completely different....I have a renewed sense of worth. I feel appreciated with the things I contribute. We created the team approach and the abundance mentality to our school and community. I feel our staff is more productive, happier. We have more fun. We are inspired and more creative because we feel better about ourselves and what we do. We feel respected. That is something we lacked before.

The following essay was written by one of my friends and colleagues when he was seventy-two years old. It is captivating for a number of reasons. The perception of a person in a leadership position steered Ronald Braithwaite away from his career path almost sixty years earlier. This is why we need to create more leaders, not more positions. Later in his life, something happened that forever changed his perception of the world that can be passed to his younger relatives. Perception in history has permanently shifted paradigms. People can see themselves in roles they previously thought not possible. After a successful career as a mechanical engineer, Ron came to us as a retiree that wanted to stay connected to a school system. He was one of the most respected employees in our district. Mr. Braithwaite was an instructional aide that engaged in every lesson for the success of his students. He cared about every person, and they responded accordingly. I am honored to call him my friend.

Hello. My name is Ronald Braithwaite and I am an instructional aide here at Belhaven Middle School. Almost a month has passed now since I arrived at the polling place to vote for Barack Obama. It was the National Presidential Election Day and a few minutes before 7 am - the scheduled opening; I was the first person in line.

Around my waist, hidden under my jacket I wore a plastic sheath that contained photographs of many of my deceased relatives. When I was motioned to come forward to vote I was so keyed up I could hardly control myself. I nervously signed and processed-in as tears of joy rolled down my cheeks. Within the voting machine - curtain drawn - I did what I came to do - cast my vote for the very first

African-American to be president of the United States of America, and this moment too, shared symbolically with my deceased relatives, and many more who had not survived to see this day. It was a moment of ultimate pride - a rush of extreme elation.

Before this day had ended the results were in; Barack Obama had won by an overwhelming margin. He was the new president-elect. Well now, I thought, I can tell my grandchildren, 'You too, can be president someday. You can be anything you want to be!'... all with complete sincerity.

Fifty-seven years ago my high school counselor steered me away from a career as an architect; not for blacks I was told. The pain of oppression, humiliation and rejection shall no longer be a black parent's greatest fear, as they hope and do their best to protect, to shield their children going out into the world.

So, Obama will be our new President come January 20th, 2009. On a platform of 'change' he was elected by a huge majority - Whites, Hispanics, Asians, Blacks, Native Americans - and he will be president to all...for all. And most significantly, Obama's election has also grossed world-wide approval and acceptance, which will help ease foreign relations.

Our Constitution's promise of equal rights for all may now be redeemed - as many nations of the world have seen the U.S. as hypocritical in its discriminatory treatment of African-Americans and others. Americans and the wide-world seemingly welcome a kept promise. And so, too, with Obama there can be pride, hope, and change.

Ron's hope is that there would be a shift in perception. How about when a woman wins an election? Or anyone that will allow a person to see themselves in a positive light. It is the same with leadership. When people see who they are and who they can become BAM! Shift happens. *Fired Up* Leadership happens.

People start to believe in themselves and the leadership process. Stakeholders want to be a part of it. They want a voice. Give them one then turn up the volume!

Let's face it, it is easier to complain than to do something and make your organization a place where everyone wants to be. It might take change and people are reluctant to change even if it's a small event. Get started with unconditional communication.

When was the last time you had a truly authentic conversation with someone and you actually listened to what they had to say? It takes practice to understand what the person is saying and be able not to interrupt and wait for your turn to speak.

Be cognizant that you are communicating every second of every day. When you are in a constructive communication zone, you'll know it. Look around. Are you where you want to be? If not, do something about it. Don't be a *Looky Loo*, someone who sits back, complains, but does nothing. They get in the way of the rest of us making progress. Choose to be a better communicator, and you will be a better communicator. Make your organization Visible, Tangible, Walk-aroundable (V, T, W) in a positive way.

SUMMARY

Practice all areas of communication. If you want to be a great public speaker, then practice. Even when you think you are great at it; you need to keep practicing. Never become complacent in any area of communication. Stay balanced in all areas. Always be a self-communicator and a listener. Keep telling yourself what you want to achieve. You are capable of remarkable accomplishments. Your students and colleagues are, too. Give them opportunities.

WE SEE THE WORLD NOT AS IT IS BUT AS WE ARE OR AS WE ARE CONDITIONED TO SEE IT

Stephen R. Covey

---

most important factor that will contribute to your leadership style is YOU. Your experiences have given you a view of the world. Before you can change anything, start with yourself. Dig deeply into your body, mind, heart, and spirit. Balance in the "whole person" approach is your biggest ally. This is also an excellent tactic for teaching. Because you understand self-care, you become more effective at teaching to the whole child and the whole person.

Take the following survey. If you score less than three in any area, target that specific area for

---

improvement. Your total score serves as a benchmark.

THE 2ND DOMAIN SURVEY COMMUNICATION AND LISTENING

1=Never 2=Sometimes 3=Frequently 4=Always

I can work independently.
1   2   3   4

I can work with a group.
1   2   3   4

I am comfortable speaking in front of people.
1   2   3   4

I like to write (in journals and essays).
1   2   3   4

I like to teach new skills to people.
1   2   3   4

I practice becoming a great listener.
1   2   3   4

THE THIRD DOMAIN

CRITICAL THINKING, PROBLEM-SOLVING, AND TEAM BUILDING

We must always consider someone else's point of view especially when it doesn't agree with ours. Everyone should feel valued. Start practicing this concept as soon as possible. The approach you take to becoming a change agent will be more impactful and genuine.

Though we may see situations from another's perspective, we cannot assume they will automatically see our point of view. We can't expect anything in return. We must consider and value everyone's opinion. Our success in certain areas will be met in a timelier manner. It takes practice, we must start now.

When you take a look at the title of the third domain, it becomes a wealth of interests, paradigms, and passions. As educators, we have been taught our whole careers to differentiate teaching and learning. It is the same with problem-solving and team-building.

LEARN

When we stop learning, we stop leading. *Fired Up* Leaders are constantly educating themselves. We are in search of knowledge. We frequently review the literature, take classes, teach, attend conferences, and learn from each other. If we are reviewing a topic that is directly related to the success of our organization, action research also becomes a component.

For instance, as educators we continually look for better ways of teaching and learning to allow our students and colleagues to reach then expand their potential. After reviewing the literature for different ways of professional development, we found that only certain methods were most effective with our professional staff. Colleagues were encouraged to attend, facilitate, and turn-key training. When it was possible, we brought experts to our school.

Rather than always using the most popular methods, we differentiated professional development just as we would teaching strategies for the students. We increased our engagement and people were creating their own leadership roles.

Likewise, the people you associate with create a knowledge base that you may not have. Their experiences and training will greatly increase ideas and "no box" thinking. More ideas create more options. Keep bringing non-traditional thinkers to the leadership table.

People are unique in some ways and alike in so many others. Your experiences, learning, and teaching styles are just as important as published research. Your action research becomes the published research. Be a learner and a leader. Find the strengths of the people around you. Then you can maximize your *Fired Up* Leadership success in the long-term.

We all have a plethora of knowledge at the end of our fingertips. I mean this literally. You can look anything up on your smartphone then disseminate that information to your entire organization seamlessly. Just make sure it is legitimate. Sometimes it helps significantly to triangulate your data to make an informative decision. I think that is where a lot of people get hung up. They rely on partial information.

Be a keen observer. If you really want to learn a lot about life, observe children. They are born without boundaries, and they offer terrific insight. Instead of telling you what you want to hear, they tell you the truth. The truth always works in the long run even if there are consequences to your opinion. Only after they are influenced by adults, do children become less free about their opinions. This is when their bias begins. Never stifle the creativity of our youth. Sometimes, we may even need to think like a child, have no boundaries.

PROBLEM SOLVING

The first step with problem solving is to identify the problem. After you identify the problem, eliminate yourself as a barrier. For instance, some people have glitches because they create them in their own minds. They look at threats and weaknesses without considering the opportunities and strengths. When you look at all internal and external factors, consider every educated solution to the problem. With every conflict, there comes opportunity.

> # THE BEST WAY TO SOLVE A PROBLEM IS NOT TO HAVE ONE. CHANGE CREATES OPPORTUNITIES TO LEARN

If you still have a problem, then you can proceed. What is the problem? Is it definitive? If it is, state the problem and do an analysis. List the opportunities (outside your organization and you), and the strengths (inside your organization and you). Now you must list the threats (outside your organization and you), and the weaknesses (inside your organization and you). Compare the two sides.

What are your possible solutions? There should be more than one. Which one is the most feasible? Now come up with a plan. This plan will be important. Your strengths will be the team's strengths. The same is true with the rest of your team. Likewise, use your strengths to devour the weaknesses. Your available resources and monetary situation will have an effect on your plan of action.

TEAM BUILDING

Team building can be tricky for a number of reasons. There is an abundance of information out there on numerous media sites. A lot of information is free and relevant. Also understand that a large number of activities can be cliché and overrated. When planning, one of the biggest components will be: "Know your audience." During the pandemic of 2020, we are discovering: "Know your delivery point."

Everything you do may not appeal to your entire audience or every participant but you can gear your activities to appeal to the majority. Know your goals for the meeting, day, month, and year. What are you trying to accomplish? For the most part, it's probably trust and collegiality.

If at all possible, when you are planning for your entire team, department or leadership group, take them off site as a bonding experience. When they are at your main campus, hundreds of distractions exist, and your team may remain guarded. Accumulate research about what worked during certain situations and fine-tune the process. Accentuate new beginnings with team-building. For instance, start your new year or new project with a field trip. Create a renaissance. Announce a new theme and service-learning platform then dig right in. If you go to an offsite location, have a scavenger hunt or go to a place of service. Food is always good, and you don't need a hefty budget.

One year, we had inclement weather so we had to do everything onsite but we kept it moving. The guest speaker we scheduled couldn't make it either. Be prepared.

This is an example of an onsite retreat: First, we introduced our new theme "School Rocks!" Then we video conferenced with our guest speaker to announce our service learning: renewable energy. We proceeded with a short meeting to do some housekeeping and raise our level of awareness. This particular year, we created a stimulating video to jumpstart our day. We included as many recent pictures of our building and people that we could find. We promoted our goals then tied it to the Olympics that just ended. It was easy to find encouragement in some of the Olympic pictures and connect the visuals to hard work, commitment, and "whatever it takes."

Later in the day, people were ready to eat. Replenish their bodies as well as spirits. Be sensitive to any allergies and beliefs. We let people know in advance what we were making. It was nice to communicate on a level that didn't involve mostly work-related jargon. The room should be filled with laughter and merriment.

For another team-building activity, we divided our large group into different "rock groups." Each participant got a "backstage pass" with a number on the back; the number designated their group. Now we had teams for our competition/team-building. We used a big dry erase board in the front of the room for a visual and to keep score. The first task was to name your "rock group." It was hilarious and interesting as each group sent a representative on stage to announce the names.

The next task was to brainstorm ideas for our service project. The teams wrote the ideas on big paper and taped it to the wall. We put a time limit on this to keep it moving. After time was called, each group read their ideas. We then moved to the gymnasium. We had music set up to greet everyone. First up was the "Rock Star Relay." Each group (band) competed against each other dressing up, running to mid-court then tagging the next person to do the same. There were many photo opportunities during this one. We finished the competition with "Name That Tune." We had several categories. Each team had a representative. The facilitator played a tune until someone guessed it. We went back to the auditorium and tallied the points. Our closing ceremony was complete with a medal themed ceremony and the national anthem. We debriefed and tied everything together. It's funny how some people remembered working in a place that wasn't fun. Granted, I can guarantee you that some people were not as enthusiastic as I was, but for the most part, everyone felt appreciated, connected, and inspired!

There are many approaches you can take to meetings and gatherings. Some approaches need to be direct and the information may not be fun material. However, we were driven to create a place where everyone wanted to be. Flexibility played a big part in the day but we were prepared. It worked. Check out Appendix A in the back of the book. Any activities that you use should be molded to your situation and organization.

Some activities you do become traditions. You must fine-tune them every year. This is a reflection from a student about an event that included parents, staffulty, students, and the community.

I had so much fun at Almost Anything Goes last night. We work so well together no matter who we are with. At AAG, everyone was with new people. Right from the start my team was stretching, talking, making up names, cheers, and figuring out plans. As we looked around the room, every team was together and talking, I was so happy to see our school as one big, happy family. I have always wanted to make a change in people's lives. That is what you do each and every day. Thank you for all your determination and courage to make this school a great place to be. I love every single renaissance event. You rock!

Almost Anything Goes is an annual nighttime event our school had. We packed our gymnasium with ten teams that performed quirky relay races and activities. The culmination is an obstacle course where the team captain gets a shaving cream pie in the face. The purpose is team-building, connections, and fun.

One of the funniest sights is the opening "act", The Balloon Break Relay. Balloons are filled with helium and tied to chairs. Each team runs the length of the floor, grabs a balloon, and sits on it to burst it. Then the team member races back across the floor to tag the next person. The funniest contestants are the smallest people because they do not know how to break the balloon. It makes some hilarious times to spend with your coworkers to prove we can all laugh at ourselves.

The following email was from a first-year teacher. He connected with the students in various ways. One way was his affection for the earth as a science teacher. He is also a lifeguard and a surfer. Many of the students surfed, too. Team-building builds relationships.

I just wanted to let you know how much I enjoy working here. I have no doubt that this school is much better off for having you here. I know the staffulty will agree with me, as I often hear them sharing the same sentiments. They all enjoy having you as their principal but maybe not as much as me. It would not be nearly as much fun if it wasn't for your enthusiasm for our school's climate and the various activities we share with the kids, community, and the staffulty. I respect your willingness to do things a little differently. Your hard work and dedication do not go unrecognized.

I have been blessed to speak to schools and facilitate workshops all over North America. Continually, I fine-tune the process. There are certain staples that I use because they are met with positive responses over and over. The school where I worked as a principal is close to the beach. During our Leadership Exchanges, workshops, and speaking engagements, I started to use a beach ball. As people enter the room, I hand them a beach ball. I ask them to write one word that describes leadership to them on the ball then pass it to someone else. At the end of the session, I collect the ball and hold it up. I have collected over 10,000 words. Overwhelmingly the number one quality of a leader is some form of character.

Many of the activities I discuss or list in the back of the book can be done virtually. As we sit in a current global pandemic, I get many questions about team building remotely. The beachball can be passed and words added virtually on social media with a unique hashtag. Be creative. You will be amazing.

TEAM WORK

Never underestimate yourself or the people around you. Never feel too powerful or too disempowered to participate. When you look at chipping in to get things done, it doesn't matter who gets the credit. Our first day of the new school year, we celebrated with outright engagement of the entire facility.

> # IT IS BETTER TO HAVE ONE PERSON WORKING WITH YOU THAN THREE WORKING FOR YOU.
> *Dwight Eisenhower*

Because I worked in a school, the first day of the new year for us was always in early September. Not only did we like to get the students excited to return to our building but we wanted everyone to connect with a new beginning, a strong start.

Remember, in the previous section how our employees started their new year, now, the whole school celebrates. We did a lot of similar activities for the students that we did for the employees. Always begin with music, enthusiasm, and lots of smiles. Make everyone feel welcome. The last class to arrive in the auditorium was always our upperclassmen. We rolled out the red carpet and gave them a standing ovation. After the national anthem, we count in the new year. Since we had a rock theme that year, we struck a gong rather than drop a ball. It's similar to the Times Square New York celebration on the traditional New Year. It's a great starting point.

This email from a teacher sums up our culture after an event that became a tradition.

I received the nicest compliment last night, and it is because of the abundance of leadership. The person told me that, 'I wished I loved my job as much as you do. You are so happy and excited when you talk about your students and the fun activities you do.' Thank you for all you do for me, our school, and community to make us better individuals.

Everyone feels a part of what we do. I remember when I almost quit after my first year teaching social studies. You helped me through a difficult time. Have a great day and keep smiling.

EMPOWER OTHERS TO BE LEADERS

When everyone in your school feels empowered, problem solving and the team approach become proactive. People feel creative, important, and action oriented. Great thinkers become great doers.

One of the most rewarding events I experience as an educator occurs when I reconnect with a former student. On one occasion, a young man came by our school for a visit. At the time, he was a sophomore at Gettysburg College. He was a committed scholar, leader, and athlete. Since I've known him, most of our conversations revolved around basketball and leadership. That afternoon was no different. He brought me up to speed on his academic career and the basketball team at Gettysburg College. Most intriguing to me was the effort he made to apply and then get accepted into a program at the Garthwait Leadership Center at the college.

His conversation was flattering to our school because he connected some of the leadership concepts we instilled in the students at an early age to the concepts at the Garthwait Leadership Center. We spoke specifically about the leadership trait of empowerment. He reflected on his time at our school and how at an early age he understood the value of being empowered and empowering others to take creative risks and experience leadership.

Coincidentally, when he came for his visit, I was engaged in an activity with a group of seventh- and eighth-graders. We were engrossed in scooping ice cream for a social later that night. He was able to recall the character he experienced as a middle schooler. The short of it is that this group of devoted middle schoolers facilitated the planning and execution of a school/community event that attracted 400 people and connected the community to our school.

When we went back to my office, he asked me how long I worked in my present position as principal. He wanted to know how I kept my energy level up for all of those years. The answer to the energy level was this, "When former students come back to our school, they keep me engaged and inspired. It comes full circle. When I see someone that took our concepts and made a commitment to hard work, it makes all the difference in the world for me to continue in this capacity. When former students talk about empowering others through leadership because they were empowered, that keeps my mission headed in the right direction. It's the strongest form of leadership that I can pass on."

This is an email from his mom after his visit.

Thanks for your email! You SHOULD be proud of him! You are personally responsible for introducing him to the magic of leadership! I cannot thank you enough for the interest you took in his development. Your influence did not end after he left Belhaven. To this day, he speaks of you very often and remains your biggest fan! Whenever anyone asks him about his interest in leadership, he always gives you high praise for creating the interest.

I am happy to tell you that the company he interned with in Washington, DC this summer formally offered him a job when he graduates! How great is that?! His hard work is definitely paying off. He was only home a few days this summer as he returned to Gettysburg two weeks early to work with the Garthwaite Leadership College program.

I truly cannot thank you enough for being such a positive influence on both of our children. Both have embraced what they learned about leadership at Belhaven and turned it into careers! WOW!! Can you imagine what lies ahead for them?

I hope you take GREAT pride in knowing that you are truly CHANGING lives for the students who are lucky enough to know you. You have truly made a huge difference in the lives of my children and I am forever grateful!

We can call that a *WOW!* Factor and a magical *tada* moment. Although she seems to give me the credit, the kudos go to the climate and culture that all stakeholders, including parents and the community put into the importance of leadership.

EMPOWERMENT WILL MAKE QUANTUM LEAPS IN ANYONE'S ABILITY TO BE A LEADER

Many people cannot share power especially if they are in an authoritative position. Positional power does not readily translate into anyone's ability to lead. Rather it is a position that can be abused or mishandled by many.

Take a look in any classroom or boardroom. Does the teacher or other executive allow the students or participants to become facilitators? If they do, chances are the other people are engaged, and they are taken to higher levels of learning and leading. Share the wealth. Share the power. Some people are under the impression that there can only be one leader in the classroom, the building, the business, the school, the district. I guarantee you those schools or organizations operate at lower capacity than those organizations that understand the value of creating leaders through empowerment.

I have worked in schools and other organizations where top authoritative positions hoard the power. These places will never be successful in the long run until they understand the concept of empowerment to create more leaders. If they do not, a collegial environment is not possible. Keeping control will not achieve organizational goals in the long run. Not only is selfishness boring but it hinders creativity. People will not be compelled to take creative risks. Likewise, there is no synergy when people hoard the power because people do not want to *go above and beyond* an average day. Importantly, in successfully empowered environments, people promote and share ideas as well as power.

Remember that when we understand the consequences for failure then we can improve and move on without a fear of taking a new creative risk. In a school, the price of our failure is the failure of our students. However, through promoting leadership from the top to the bottom then back up to the top, taking a creative risk doesn't feel like a risk, especially when we empower one another. The same rings true in any organization. When people are hindered because of disempowerment, few members feel connected. People feel unimportant when they are not allowed to be creative through leadership. Do not let the "U-Boat Captains" disempower you. A "U-Boat Captain" is someone that sits in the back of the lounge and pulls down the periscope every time a new or different idea comes along. Because your idea may be away from the "norm" or it may take some work, they shoot it down. Do not let the U-Boat Captains interrupt your mission under any circumstance. Let them know how you feel. Be empowered; feel empowered; empower others!

THE BLAME GAME

A lot of people do it. People play it because it is easy to play. This is a common barrier in anyone's ability to lead and become successful. Let's say the *LeaderShip* runs into an iceberg. There will be a lot of blame to go around. Immediately people won't shoulder the blame so they start blaming anyone but themselves. These toxic and volcanic personalities can be eliminated if your decision-making process includes all stakeholders.

It takes a certain attitude to create a positive culture, and you need to reinforce your vision and mission continually. Positive culture is synonymous with positive leadership. You have to spread more positive than negative. The scales will be swayed through hard work, commitment, and trust. Passionate people win every time because the domains are driven by their passion to succeed.

SUMMARY

Any time you are solving a problem for the greater good of your organization, look at it from everyone's "point-of-view." Unconditional leadership is a lot like unconditional love; do not expect anything in return. Without love there is no leadership. Empower the people around you to become leaders and generate multiple ideas. Include the heretics, outliers, disruptors, and great thinkers in your leadership opportunities. Bring your students to other schools and conferences. Allow them to facilitate and share. Invite other schools to your building. Never underestimate the collective power of your team. Some call it synergy. It causes long-term success. Your legacy lives on long after you leave.

Take the following survey. If you score less than three in any area, target that specific area for improvement. Your total score serves as a benchmark.

THE 3RD DOMAIN SURVEY
CRITICAL THINKING, PROBLEM - SOLVING, AND TEAM BUILDING

1=Never 2=Sometimes 3=Frequently 4=Always

I consider different points of view.
1   2   3   4

I generate ideas from multiple sources.
1   2   3   4

I have attended leadership training at my school or workplace.

1 2 3 4

I learn from professionals outside of my organization.

1   2   3   4

I participate in a club, sport, band, and/or community organization.

1   2   3   4

I can facilitate a team-building activity.

1   2   3   4

THE FOURTH DOMAIN

CHARACTER AND SERVICE

he *Fired Up* domains are essential components of leadership. Domain 4 is no different.

CHARACTER TRAITS

When you evaluate your character, keep in mind that all character traits have opposites. If you do not possess a character trait then you might possess the opposite of that trait. For instance, if you do not have enthusiasm you have apathy. I'm sure that you can find arguments to this but what is in the middle? Just like most leadership traits are intertwined, so are most character traits.

> **NEVER TAKE THE EASIEST WAY**
> **UNLESS IT'S THE BEST WAY**

You must decide your core values that line up with your goals and mission. It is something you review frequently. Self-communicate your character just like you do your goals and plans of action. Positive character becomes a habit. Trustworthiness might be in the top ten for me.

IF PEOPLE TRUST YOU AUTHENTIC RELATIONSHIPS ARE MORE LIKELY TO EXIST

If trust is present, more can get accomplished and leadership does not take on a power position but rather a choice. Trust is influential just like all positive character traits. As fast as you can, list your favorite character traits.

How great did that feel?

Look at the traits you wrote. Will leadership be effective without the presence of those traits? Chances are it will not be. There is a strong likelihood that the same qualities for character are also effective leadership assets. Any positive character that you use in your *Fired Up*

Leadership will become an attribute to your leadership legacy. Remember, no one is perfect at character so when you make a mistake it's OK to apologize then move on in a positive direction. *"Character begins at birth and ends at death."* That gives you a lot of stimulus and response in between.

SERVICE

As mentioned previously, the power of positive self-communication can make quantum leaps in your ability to achieve some noteworthy feats. Now that you are on your way to mastering positive thinking, focus on the power of positive "doing." When you model positive behavior, and get your team involved, your influence and the influence of your organization will exceed what you thought you were capable of accomplishing.

There is a difference between community service and service learning. Most people have never really thought about it because they are too busy trying to pile up hours. Community service donates hours or some other resource to your community. There is no real learning or commitment taking place.

Service learning is actually making the connection to the community and discovering their needs. Then you follow through on satisfying that need to make the community or group better. Service learning can also be described as community involvement: a connection for the betterment of people around you. Awareness is a key factor.

Many years ago, I joined a community education foundation because I wanted to give the children of our town more opportunities for success. The president of the organization asked me if I was joining to give back. My response was, "I'm not joining to give back, I'm joining to give." Service learning is unconditional whereas community service has motive for self-gain or fulfilling an obligation. Community service sounds punitive or obligatory.

Many student groups require community service hours without the notion of a plan to make a difference. The planning part is important when formulating servant leadership. Service learning is an important component to *Fired Up* Leadership and should not be taken lightly. What are the needs of the organization or community? What are your special talents and/or the talents of your organization?

Take a long look at how you can make yourself, the people around you, and your community better. There are many opportunities for your organization to get involved and make a difference locally and globally. One year our school raised money for an organization that brings clean water systems to Chinese orphanages. Another year we sponsored a cancer support organization in our state. Other years we supported local food banks and homeless shelters. There are multiple chances to service learn. Come up with a plan and execute it.

> ## SERVICE IS A FRAME OF MIND
> ## NOT A TIME OF YEAR

When your mind is set on making a positive difference, service-learning opportunities will arise. Service contributes to a life of leadership. Put a plan in place, and your role will be obvious as your compass points in the right direction, and your *Fired Up* Leadership will be a huge difference maker.

Although your school or organization may plan a service project, sometimes the world around you may alter your plans. As your leadership ability progresses, so does your adaptability to unexpected occurrences. Your adaptability becomes part of your leadership repertoire.

As we are feeling the pain of the pandemic of 2020, the following story brings us to the realization that our reality can become altered and our direction must be changed. This can allow us to adapt to make the outcomes more positive than we imagined. Our advantage in the following story was that we already planned a service component to our year. We just redirected because we were prepared with necessary resources. This is an example of how our school refocused due to an unexpected change in our environment.

I don't know where to begin except to say that I am grateful. I am a middle school principal in New Jersey, and our school closed for three days until the power was restored in the wake of Hurricane Sandy. We are located about ten minutes from our closest Jersey shore town, Ocean City. Our city, Linwood, is surrounded by back bays and estuaries but we survived this one. During the summer we were closed for four days during a derecho, hurricane-like conditions with ferocious winds and torrential downpours. Most families lost power for a week.

All around us, schools were closed indefinitely as administrators and town officials sorted out a plan to rebuild local communities. Ten miles away in Atlantic City the casinos remained closed for five days as most of the city was still without power. We have a lot of our families that depend on the Atlantic City economy for their livelihood. Many of our staffulty (faculty and staff) were affected directly at their homes or the homes of loved ones. Selflessly, they put less fortunate people ahead of themselves as we re-aimed our service project resources.

In classes, we shifted our service-learning platform to raise money for the cleanup and restoration from the hurricane and to step up our food drive. Before the hurricane, our service-learning platform consisted of raising money for soccer balls that double as generators for lamps and charging *stations to distribute to those places that do not have power or play equipment.*

We put that on the back burner and focused on more immediate, local needs and accepted a leadership role and started spreading kindness. This was the second time in a few months a lot of our students were without electrical power, or they were displaced. Some people totally lost their homes. Some schools could not open because of structural damage or because their students were displaced.

As crazy as it sounds, these are opportunities and experiences we embraced. We must embrace them for the opportunity to serve and the opportunity to learn. We must embrace these opportunities for the chance to lead. Sometimes in education, we are bogged down with directives, reform, and bureaucracy. These moments of unrest allow us to teach and lead to the whole child. Empathy becomes more common.

As we rearranged our school calendars and lessons and redirected our resources and initiatives, we came together to make a difference in ourselves and in our community. At the end of the week, we were looking for direction as people were starting to get back to their shore homes and some sort of normalcy.

I viewed pictures, videos, and visited some areas. It was devastating to see as we became emotional when you knew the people affected. There was a plethora of coverage in the media about the American Red Cross and their need for monetary resources. I visited the closest Red Cross site to try and fill a void.

There were people there not as lucky as we were. There was a group looking for relocation that made any barrier we had pale in comparison. When it was my turn in line, the first thing the Red Cross lady said, 'I am tired.' I asked what she needed then she told me they were inundated with volunteers and couldn't disperse them where they needed to go. She said the most effective contribution would be money. She also urged us to donate to local food banks. So that's what we did.

We connected with a few schools that needed assistance. People that were affected by Hurricane Sandy were looking for direction just as the people looking for service. If you have done something to help, you are a leader. If you haven't done something to help, become a leader.

Leadership is not popularity or recognition. Effective leadership begins with service. Be an example, and I'm sure your organization will, too. You will change the world in a positive way by starting with yourself and your community. Individually, we can surely make a difference. Collectively, we can make a synergistic difference, and we will.

HONK IF YOU LOVE SOMEONE

Acts of character and service intertwine as your leadership skills progress. They become commonplace. When you think of service, never think that it has to be a monumental task. Sometimes it does take large scale planning and resources but other times it can be as easy as making a sign.

Someone sent me a link to this video.

Check out the video. It proves just how easy it can be to put a smile on someone's face, change their day, and promote positive leadership. I felt compelled to try it out at our middle school. Every other Friday, we had an advisory schedule. We shortened the regular class schedule by a few minutes to create an extra period at the end of the day. We called it an activity schedule. Each certified staffulty member had a group of students that they advised to initiate creative opportunities not in our regular curriculum.

With my advisory students, we watched the video and then replicated the project in front of our school. My face still hurts from laughing and smiling so much. We made signs similar to the ones in the video, *Honk if you love someone* and *Honk if you are happy* and  headed to the front of our school. Since I'd seen the video several weeks prior, I'd made a permanent sign to put on our sidewalk.

Within a few minutes, the students were completely invested and engaged. Cars, vans, and trucks were honking and smiling. One lady stopped, rolled down her window, and smiled ear to ear. She said, "I can't honk because I'm not happy." I said, "Then why are you smiling?" We made her day positive!

The kids were jumping up and down, waving, and spreading happiness. WOW! What a great idea. Make sure you watch the video then spread the smiles!

When students think about "paying it forward" or a service-learning project, they may reflect upon awareness of the target. This particular event is quick, easy, and anyone can duplicate it. It works!

> ## NEVER DOUBT THAT A SMALL GROUP OF THOUGHTFUL, COMMITTED CITIZENS CAN CHANGE THE WORLD. INDEED IT IS THE ONLY THING THAT EVER HAS.
>
> *Margaret Meade*

LEADERSHIP SUMMIT: LEAD THE LEADERS

When you create a leadership culture, you build a bridge and promote your school as the center of your community. Once each year, we had a

Leadership Summit. I call it "Lead the Leaders." The Summit is a two-day event where the entire school participates in leadership activities promoting the character and service components of the *Fired Up* model. Every grade level and curricular area coordinate the events. Whether it is a themed t-shirt or community partnership, each year lends itself to a new experience.

Typically, summits involved our extended community. We had service-learning trips for groups of eighth graders. Other teachers stayed at school and facilitated activities that promoted problem solving and teamwork. For example, team-building activities in physical education classes and putting together birthday bags for homeless children. We had guest speakers that were former students talking about transition to high school. They discussed their many mistakes as well as multiple successes.

Another speaker was the community outreach director from the Atlantic City Rescue Mission. She talked about the overall daily operations and the need for community members to become engaged in distributing meals and collecting clean clothes and hygiene products. This allowed our students to create service opportunities.

To integrate service into their curriculum, language arts teachers used clips of homeless children in Camden, New Jersey and their plight to find housing. Another teacher displayed a *New York Times* article that showed not so typical needy people standing in line for food. These people had previously made over $200,000 but became underemployed or jobless. The examples showed our students that perception became a different reality. Servant leadership opportunities took a different direction and formed a diversified clientele.

Some students coordinated art projects and painted our walls with murals and inspirational quotes. Another team designed and painted a leadership banner. At the end of each day, we came together in the auditorium and debriefed the day. Students and staffulty gave reports on the accomplishments or read essays or gave data on collected items. This is the shortened version. When you create your summit, use your imagination and allow the students to come up with ideas. Let them facilitate as well. When students become facilitators, it opens their leadership world to more possibilities.

Be sure to tell your participants to begin planning for the next event while ideas are fresh. What worked? What didn't work? How can you create awareness?   Immediately, our teachers start brainstorming. A video with the pictures and video clips from the day is streamed online to relive the day. *WOW!* Factor. This is something every organization should do. Remember though, this state-of-mind must be reinforced during the entire year, not just one day.

Any organization can host events like this. We proved this by taking groups of our students and staffulty to different organizations to do these types of conferences. We even visited a major energy company to give a presentation on our school leadership experiences. Their positive feedback was priceless to our stakeholders.

This is a reaction from one of their leadership team members to another employee.

Were you able to get down to the leadership presentation from the school? It was amazing. We clapped and yelled and smiled and high-fived each other. I can't wait to give a report at our next meeting.

One year, our Leadership Summit focused on diversity and gender equality. When we speak to diversity, we think about cultural diversity as well as diverse perception, thinking, gender, and a variety of topics that connect us all to each other or disengage us from each other. We certainly stirred up a lot of emotion and creative thinking that year generating some dialogue for home. We wanted those conversations to continue.

We placed a map of the world in the lobby and asked everyone in our school to stick a pin on the country to indicate their ancestry. Our school represented every continent except Antarctica. This was an icebreaker that allowed everyone to see how different and alike we are as a school.

We planned for months to get the right professional speakers, create enough activities, and make correlations to everything we were doing. We searched around the country, and found two highly recommended speakers. We were ready to stir emotions, burst bubbles, and create different ways of looking at the world.

As an educator and principal of our school, I wanted to create experiences that our students didn't have. As a parent, I wanted the students to be comfortable with who they were and make changes if they weren't.

The first speaker was intelligent, serious when he had to be, funny, and entertaining. He brought his experiences with indigenous people, hate groups, and everyday observations. He demonstrated our human ability to be manipulated, be different, and our capacity to follow our heart.

Everyone is born to think creatively without prejudice. It is only when we put parameters, negative influence, or control that their thinking stifles their progression. This creates implicit bias that we all acquire. We created a lot of dialogue that was promoted in the classes for the rest of the day. For instance, reflective writing, thank you notes, and discussion. We encouraged students to continue the discussion at home and bring their parents to the evening assembly.

The second speaker spoke to the girls about leadership and self-image. The boys had a plethora of activities that related to them. The events were set up as a nice transition from the previous day. All students participated in martial arts, team building, and small group discussion.

The boys built a remembrance tree for a local grieving support organization.

As a parent, I always initiate meaningful dialogue with my daughters. However, I get the same standard answers that you might get, *What did you do in school today? Oh, nothing. Same old stuff.* If parents are informed, we can start the dialogue differently. *I heard you had a speaker today. He travels the country and speaks to students about some sensitive subjects? It reminds me of a trip I took to another school in Arizona. Tell me more about it.*

When we had visitors and speakers at our school, I often brought my family to our school, and welcomed the visitors to our home. It was awkward at times but it definitely started a different type of conversation.

As an educator, I am thankful for the commitment and hard work of all our stakeholders in our efforts to create a whole child and today's leaders. I was always proud of our students and their efforts and reactions to our Leadership Summits.

In our exit interviews with our graduating students, there were always lasting impressions of the Leadership Summits. It is something every school leader should do to fine-tune the process of leadership.

We received a plethora of feedback from our summits. This email from a parent sums our efforts up very well.

I wanted to take a moment to thank you and whoever brought Mr. Terrell in to speak with the kids yesterday. My girls were shaken up, amazed and inspired by the speaker's powerful words.

It takes a lot for me, at times, typically cynical and jaded teenager to engage and feel moved by something or someone. One daughter could not stop talking about the way he made them all think so differently about the way we look at the world. While our other daughter, my shy girl, felt empowered enough to actually get up and speak in front of the assembly.

We feel blessed to have the girls in such an excellent school for many reasons. These out of the box experiences are some that they will take with them and always remember. Thank you for your continued dedication and enthusiasm.

CELEBRATE

Celebration is an essential component of any organization. It validates your service and character. As a society, we Americans celebrate just about anything. Why not celebrate success, collegiality, character, and service within our organizations? Whether it's school, workplace, a team, or a community group, celebrate when you achieve your goals.

> **WE DON T NEED A HERD OF CHICKENS WE NEED A TEAM OF EAGLES**

In our organization, we celebrated our collegiality that brought us together with common goals of character and service. We celebrated a strong start to the new year. We also celebrated a stronger finish at the end of the year. We had a half-left celebration midway through the year. Don't keep the great things happening in your organization a secret.

We celebrated each other. Most celebrations become traditions. If your celebrations become traditions please do not forget to fine-tune the quality to appeal to different stakeholders and different colleagues. We have a team picture each year along with a team huddle each month. The year started with a staffulty field trip. We have a leadership summit that includes two days of service and leadership activities. Leadership Olympics occur near the end of the year.

The events that make you feel great make other people feel great as well. How did you celebrate today? We held a plethora of celebrations. No one has ever said, "Hey! Stop celebrating so much!" What are you going to celebrate today? Self-communicate a celebration then spread the fun.

Positive influence can occur in some of the strangest situations. We hosted a leadership conference that included over fifty organizations. There was an abundance of breakout sessions, an opening and closing, and just fun in general.

Here is an email from one of our staffulty members.

I woke up Friday not feeling well, but knowing we were hosting the (leadership) conference gave me the strength to come into work. The pep rally was one of the best I have ever seen! The energy in the room was awesome. I was sitting and watching the smiles on everyone's face. It was priceless. Both the kids and adults all seem to enjoy every second of it. Throughout the day I heard people saying such great things about our school and our students that it almost brought tears to my eyes. I was so proud. Even in the bathroom there were teachers taking pictures (we have murals and quotes) to share with their schools when they returned. I found myself last night thinking again how truly fortunate I am to be a part of such a great school. I know it was a team effort, but none of it would have been possible without you. You are truly an inspiration to so many teachers and students.

SUPER BOWL VICTORIES

If Americans were as obsessed with education and leadership as they were with professional sports, our country would make some remarkable gains in character and service in our communities every day. I have to admit, I am one of those people stuck on my couch every Sunday during football season rooting for my favorite NFL team. It allows me to feel a part of something bigger than me. However, so does service and kindness.

At my age, it's safe to say that the window of opportunity to play professional sports has expired. I do, however, feel that events in my life will forever equate to winning the Super Bowl or a national championship or an international award of being a great "difference maker." People should never feel that they have nothing left.

It is because of the remarkable people I've met along my journey in life that stories continue to accumulate. When people go further to accomplish more than they thought possible, that is a Super Bowl victory for me. This is one of my connections to character and service. We must keep people believing in not only who they are but who they can become.

Earlier in this book, you read a poem by my former student, Julie. Over the years we've kept in touch as she progressed through high school, college, and her current vocation as a teacher. She wrote the foreword to this book. Humbled and proud I am about that. Reread it while it is fresh on your mind.

When she came back to the area for the holidays Julie always visited our school. We had her as our keynote on one of our first days for staffulty. She spoke to classes on leadership days. For Julie, the tipping point occurred when she looked in the mirror and not only saw who she was but saw who she could become. We believed in her, and she believed in herself. She knew the value and sacrifice of hard work and commitment. After one visit, we were walking back to the front of the building, and she said, *"I don't know if I ever told you Dr. R. but you really made a difference in my life."* *WOW!* Factor.

Every educator wants to make a difference. As Julie told me those words, I thought of all the other educators that continue to make a positive difference. For all those times you hear those words, keep in mind that there are thousands of times you never do but those words are said about you and people you know. If you are an educator, thank you for entering the noblest profession on earth (and beyond). If you are any professional, thank a teacher!

The parent of a former student called to let me know that her son was being recognized as a high school football All American. Only ninety students from across the country are invited by the United States Army to participate in a prestigious bowl game that honors them as the nation's top players.

His mother told me that after he left our middle school, he frequently talked about his positive experiences and leadership opportunities that were afforded to him during his time  at our school. She attributed his success to his experiences and leadership opportunities that started in middle school. (I think parenting played a part just as important).

Dr. R. Thanks so much for coming. I didn't really have a chance to thank you for everything. I wouldn't be where I am today if it wasn't for you instilling the traits into me that you did while I was at Belhaven (Middle School). You meet a handful of special people in your life that make an impact on you and you're definitely one of those people for me. ~Jimmy

Jimmy and I have stayed connected over the years. He went to Temple University on a full athletic scholarship then transferred to Wagner University for his final two years of eligibility to earn a master's degree. While I was writing this piece for the book, I reached out to see how he was doing. After his graduation from college, his recent marriage and the birth of his son, I asked how leadership connected to his success in life. Jim has an MBA and is working towards a Ph. D. He presently works as a network manager for a major health organization.

One thing that leadership has taught me over the years is that you need to arrive at the realization that each and every one of your shortcomings will eventually open opportunities for you that you never dreamed possible. Furthermore, those realizations will lead to optimism and even appreciation during tough times with the understanding and gratitude of the lessons that will be learned along the way when facing adversity.

My colleagues and I recently interviewed Jim on our Facebook Live show, *The Empower Half Hour*, Episode 22. He spoke about his leadership journey that started in middle school and still continues. He could always make me laugh as a middle school student and he still makes me laugh as a twenty-six-year-old. On the show, Jim candidly portrayed his experiences as the number one place kicker in the country and ensuing events at two different Division 1 universities as a football player. His approach allowed him to find his inner strength and steer him towards his future. His story continues to be absolutely compelling.

His connection to life and leadership is a *WOW! Factor*, magical *tada* moment, and definitely a Super Bowl Victory for all of Jimmy's teachers. For me, it started with his commitment to character and the opportunities for servant leadership. Every time I think of Jimmy, I smile. He impacted our school as a positive force just as hundreds of other students did because they rose to higher levels of their passion through leadership. He makes the connections of the trials and tribulations that life throws at you. He realizes the importance of opportunity and opportunity cost. His best is yet to come.

I get it...where I am today has a lot to do with my time spent in middle school. Those are important years, very impactful. Twice last week at the drive through, I bought the person's order behind me. I wouldn't have done it if I didn't hear you preaching it.~Jim Cooper

This email from a parent gives us another opportunity to reflect on the importance of giving our students time and space to grow and find their paths.

Graduation was terrific; a great sendoff for the class. We just wanted to drop you a line and extend our thanks for all your efforts with our son and his classmates over the last 4 years.

Your enthusiasm, encouragement and just being there for a handshake or a pat on the back (not to mention the inspirational messages from Yoda) have benefitted all of the kids, but we know firsthand the impact it has had on John.

He has grown greatly over the last four years and no doubt the atmosphere that you and all involved at Belhaven have created has contributed greatly to his growth. You hit it right on the head last night when you spoke about Belhaven being different and citing the energy at the school.

Any great organization has great leadership and we as a community are very fortunate to have you setting the tone at the top which allows the school to thrive the way it does.

While our son is moving on, we are happy that we still have (our daughter) at school so we can hang around for a couple of more years.
~Grateful Parents

Most of these stories can impact any of the Five Domains because the domains are interconnected. An act of positive character can make a huge difference in someone's day. What you throw out there eventually comes back. Today, it may be coffee and a donut that changed a trajectory. Tomorrow, it may be a paradigm shift that changes implicit bias for a better perception and understanding of the human race. I keep preaching: leadership is not a one-time event.

> ## THE ONLY PEOPLE TO GET EVEN WITH ARE THOSE THAT HAVE HELPED YOU
> *Anonymous*

SUMMARY

There will always be a timeless correlation to leadership, service, and character. Be that person you want around you. Always be grateful and never forget to celebrate the success of your organization.

Any positive leadership will contain service. The most important component of service is awareness and authenticity. It is not the number of hours you serve but the impact. Share your stories and encourage other people to share theirs.

Take the following survey. If you score less than three in any area, target that specific area for improvement. Your total score serves as a benchmark.

THE 4TH DOMAIN SURVEY
CHARACTER AND SERVICE

1=Never 2=Sometimes 3=Frequently 4=Always

People in our organization are polite.
1   2   3   4

I practice positive character daily.

1   2   3   4

I have participated in community and/or school service projects.

1   2   3   4

I can facilitate a service-learning project.

1   2   3   4

What are your essential qualities of a leader:

THE FIFTH DOMAIN

PASSION

When you create a culture of leadership, you discover a culture of passion. That is the center of *Fired Up* Leadership. When you consciously follow your passion, you give other people permission to pursue their passion - you empower people to go places they never thought possible. At different points in your life, your fire may dim, then someone walks into your life that shows you the endless possibilities you bring to the world. And it becomes reciprocal.

PASSION BEATS DATA EVERY TIME

In the following image, you'll see the first four domains are continually feeding off of each other.

The Fifth Domain, passion, constantly fuels the fire to keep your flame lit in the other domains. As you pursue balance in your life and leadership, the five domains become complimentary. Balance is the key.

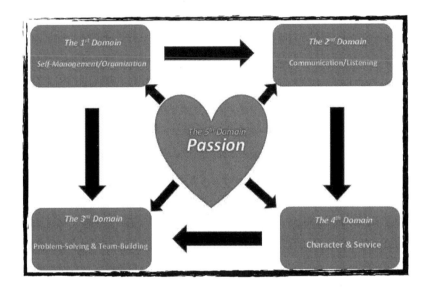

Your *Fired Up* Leadership enables you to spark change. Your passion can do just that. This is your call to disrupt. Your unique talents will contribute to what the world needs: You! This is not a moment. It is a movement. You will attract people with a like mindset that will get things done instead of just talking about what you can do. People have different passions. Encourage it!

Have you ever wondered why two people in the same house with the same resources with the same parents have totally different success? How about the person sitting next to you? How about the person in the next room? We were not all born on a level playing field. Maybe, some of it is chance, resources, or IQ, or maybe someone chose to disrupt the status quo.   I did and so should you! It does not start tomorrow, disruption starts now.

If you are truly passionate about something, other people will feel it.

> # YOUR PASSION SETS YOUR SOUL AND HEART ON FIRE

You wake up thinking about it. You go to bed thinking about it. You start living that *Fired Up* life. Your *WOW!* Factors *and Magical tada moments* appear every day because you create them every day.

When I was the principal of a middle school, there was not one stakeholder unaware of my passion for education. I was excited to get there, and the students were, too. Students and the staffulty had abundant chances to examine the limitless options that life presents. Walk into any school. You do not have to ask what kind of school it is. You know immediately.

Embedded in the curriculum of instruction, students were given outlets to become inventors to pursue their passions, and they gladly accepted. A sixth-grade student invented a solution for a lockdown safety feature. Think about that. *WOW!* Factor.

If a teacher can inspire a sixth grader to invent a legitimate device that was a game changer, then all educators must allow themselves to display their passion so people see themselves differently. It allows people to go against the grain and discover who they are. We had eighth graders invent, design, and produce gadgets that generated energy: surfboard fins, skateboard wheels, locker doors, and my favorite, a toilet paper dispenser.

We had a STEAM (Science, Technology, Engineering, Arts, Science) Career Fair one year with over a hundred adults that followed their passions as a career. The students saw people of all ages, races, religions, and genders excited about what they did. They also saw traditional and nontraditional careers as a path to explore their fire. Some students were even invited to shadow a professional for a day. *WOW!* Factor

A simple act can make a big difference. During my principalship, I stood at the side of the street and blasted music and held up signs: "You are amazing." "You Rock." "Get *Fired Up.*" "You are beautiful." "Have a beautiful day." The students and parents expected me to be there in rain, snow, cold, and heat. And I was there. It promoted peace, love, and joy.

During my last week at the school, all the students lined the street with positive messages on signs. *WOW!* Factor. They got  me. They felt my passion and I felt theirs.

I participated in every rally and contest. I got on the roof dressed in costumes. I made an opening day video every year. I painted our vision and mission on the wall, twenty feet high. Maybe, if I compared what we did to other schools, it would be unique. For me, it just felt right and it was part of my leadership style. We did what we needed to remain exemplary academically. We also did what we

needed to remain balanced socially and emotionally. The following reflection from a colleague is a nice summation.

When Frank started with us at Belhaven he had a vision. Leadership and community were priorities. He recognized that no one person could make changes or do it all, and he went to work building teams, encouraging staff to explore their passions. Strong teams share their strengths, they collaborate and celebrate to make things happen... He has done some crazy things to ensure his vision and to continue to excite everyone. We have been on a Jedi mission, sang with Elvis, and watched a superhero fly across the stage. He has invited us all on his journeys...I have always admired the way Frank encouraged leadership at all levels. He encouraged and found ways for staffulty and students to explore their passions and to achieve. This is what has made Belhaven unique!

We had dozens of students that surfed and skateboarded. They were very passionate about it. One of our many service projects included collecting clean socks for the Atlantic City Rescue Mission. Our plan was to skateboard down the bike path and collect socks. The students told me that if I skated, they would collect one thousand pairs of socks. A colleague built me a long-board (low and slow) and I learned. We collected over two thousand pairs of socks! I will never forget that experience and neither will the students. I still ride my longboard. I get a lot of strange looks but I enjoy it. Everyone knew it was alright to have fun and pass your passion for

teaching and learning. We brought another skate day inside the school on account of rain. It was amazing! Within minutes, we had twenty-five students. Some of the students had never attended an after school event. WOW! A great way to think differently. It was a wonderful connector to what we do. The students thought it was the coolest thing ever to skate through the hallways. I did, too! Sometimes you have to go with your gut.

One of my daily goals was to walk through every classroom every day. As busy as I was on some days, just a minute sometimes made a big difference. The students and teachers were used to it. If I missed a day, or I was not in the building, they knew. When you show up every day, they expect you. If you come once in a while, people think something is wrong.

STRONG VISIBILITY BECAME A STAPLE OF LEADERSHIP

It was the visibility of all staffulty members that solidified a part of our culture that contributed to safety and caring.

One day, I was in our engineering class. We started a conversation about the qualities of a leader. The students, teacher, and I started to come up with core words. One student had a suggestion to write them on a surfboard. Amazing idea!! We started right away!

The next time we had a group of students from another school, we copied surfboards on paper. Each participant wrote a leadership trait on their board. On the back, they wrote a letter to a person that possessed that quality and why. Over the years it evolved into surfboards you can wear around your neck. Just like that, Core Boards were born. After doing it hundreds of times, it really built relationships about topics that students and educators are passionate about. We even donated money to nonprofits by selling them. *WOW!* Factor.

This quick note from a parent let us know that when we commit to her children, we are on the same page.

Just wanted to take a minute to let you know how grateful we feel to have you as the heart and soul of Belhaven. The culture you and the teachers have created is better than we could have imagined....the energy, enthusiasm, and excitement you bring is almost enough to make us want to go back to middle school. Oh, and we didn't know you skateboarded.

CHOOSE YOUR LIFE BEFORE IT CHOOSES YOU

Most people have dreams. They dream of a reality beyond their expectations. When you see yourself differently, and you begin to take yourself to higher levels of leading and learning, goals become real. You start catching the dreams you are chasing.

I talk about Super Bowl victories all the time because we can experience those *WOW!* Factors our entire life. Is there a pinnacle? There probably is not for me and there should not be for you either.

I've heard people discuss the over-importance people put on happiness. That is absolutely crazy. Happiness is not the only component to life but it certainly needs to be a resounding factor. You cannot make it a one-time event. Happiness does not happen nonstop but everyone should experience it every day.

I've never woken up and said, "This day is going to be soooo mediocre." Neither should you.

Granted, there are times to be sad, but one of my goals is to be happy. I want my wife and daughters to be happy. I want you to wake up with gratitude and happiness, too. Yes, I am putting an emphasis on happiness.

You will have more than one passion. I have accumulated many over the years. There were times when a certain passion became a part of me. Whether it was basketball, magic, education, leadership, organizational culture, or family. It defined me and contributed to my legacy. One factor of your legacy is that it starts at birth and ends at death. It's branding that you control.

Students came back to visit our middle school all the time. Many came at a time when they were pursuing their passion as a career. On one return trip, a student told me that he was pursuing his passion of football at the collegiate level. He was recruited to play baseball at his former college but came to the realization that his journey needed to be redirected. He played Division One football at Temple University in Philadelphia. Upon graduation, he continued to follow his passion for football as a professional football scout. The student, Tommy, understood the connection that passion played in driving his leadership. He sums it up beautifully.

Find the thing you can't live without and fully commit to it with everything you have. For me, that's always been football. It won't be easy, but the feeling of knowing you're being true to yourself makes it all worth it.

After congratulating him for accepting a job with a professional football team, he said, *"Thank you, Dr. R! I'm still using all the principles YOU taught us over a decade ago."*

We had students that followed their passion for careers in music, teaching, technology, and service among many other opportunities. I believe that by encouraging creativity and differentiating according to passion and with passion might have allowed some students to catch their dreams. One of the best moments I have as an educator is to see this play out to fruition.

Literally the day before I am typing this, I received a CD in the mail that contained an album from a former student. Not only did it put the biggest smile on my face but I listened to it at loud volume and could not stay in my seat. Visualize that: an old guy at a traffic light, dancing in his car. I totally enjoyed it. And yes, I know I could have just downloaded the music but it was special to hold it in my hand and post it on social media. Check it out @trafficandtransit! Awesome job, Devon!

RELATIONSHIP BUILDING

Differentiate according to passion. Think about how powerful that can be. My whole life as an educator, I never thought about differentiating instruction according to a student's or an adult's passion. Once I saw it, it became common sense. I witnessed the power of passion in teenagers, young adolescents, and children. As students are able to facilitate learning to other students, an amazing thing happens. They find a new direction to see who they could become.

As part of a normal observation, I visited a social studies class. The lesson was a component of the American Civil War unit. The assessment was project based by choice. A student went to the front of class to make a presentation about baseball during the Civil War era. Baseball was his passion. His presentation was outstanding. From that day forward, the student was a different person. He was always smiling and eager to talk to his teachers and peers. They were anxious to interact with him, too. He became a database for a game everyone liked, baseball. He had a new persona that included being connected.

The following is an excerpt from a student who was asked to sum up his time in our school.

Each morning, rain or shine, Dr. R. stands outside playing music and holding up signs like "Honk if you're happy." Because of his enthusiasm, our students are excited about coming to school. Every day, he walks the halls greeting and interacting with students and staffulty. He works his hardest to create a happy, safe environment for everyone in the school.

Dr. R. taught us time and time again that bullying is wrong. Every year he comes up with a lesson that he hopes will inspire us to be the best we can be. He encourages students to be upstanders, positive role models, and leaders. Our school is epic, not ordinary. Without Dr. R., we would not have a school that is the heart of the community. Through all the special events like movie nights, ice cream socials, dances, and service-learning projects like skate for change, our students feel like they are part of a family.

We don't realize how fortunate we are to have such an amazing school. Renaissance, advisory periods, Street Team, leadership exchanges, Almost Anything Goes, and other important aspects of this school...spirit, passion, and leadership.

Traditions and culture take time to build and it can become a positive way of life. Not everything appeals to everyone. You build anyway. I can remember the rough roads as well. The first year I became principal, I was in the cafeteria and a student jumped on a table. I'm not sure why. I asked him to get down. He said, "You f%&#@ing make me." I started building a relationship with that student immediately. I had to.

Another goal I had was to talk to the students during lunch. I rotated through the café and ate or talked to them. A novel approach when you consider most principals may not do that.

A decade later we had a bad budget year and many thereafter. In order to keep all the instructional staff, I became the lunchroom monitor. The students built me a lifeguard stand. It was awesome! I could see everyone and everyone  could see me. The students started to monitor themselves and clean their own tables. We played music frequently and danced on inclement weather days.

Each year, our education foundation held a silent auction. Two of the highest bids were always Principal for the Day and sitting on the lifeguard stand during lunch.

VOICE

Our staff and faculty were given a voice. We gave our students a voice. Because we did, they expected to use it. They facilitated workshops with each other. They trained other schools. We held conferences and they spoke, trained, and demonstrated our success. Our students went to board of education meetings. So did the adults that worked in our building.

One morning I walked into a classroom and spotted one of our students, Kurt. He had long, shaggy, blonde hair and a smile that lit up the room. He wore jeans and t-shirts. Would you have picked him out as a leader before you read this book?

He embraced his leadership opportunities early on because he made a choice to lead by example. He was a staple at our events and lived his life in a positive direction. His mother told me that I saw his light shine a lot sooner than most people. When I looked at Kurt, I always saw his potential to be a game changer.

When he was just a seventh grader, Kurt stood up in front of six hundred peers and teachers to announce: "Thank you for changing my life from an ordinary kid to a leader. You have given us more leadership training than most adults." For me, it was one of those *WOW!* Factors, a magical *tada* moment.

It made us realize that there was legitimacy in allowing all students to have leadership opportunities at an early age. Kurt's statement validated the importance of the power of choice and the power of passion. He saw himself differently. He saw who he could become.

Presently, Kurt is a Systems Engineer in a school district and getting ready to marry his high school sweetheart. His path reflects the belief he has in himself. Just as educators inspire their students, students inspire their teachers. It remains easy to find living proof of that.

Frequently, students would come to me or their teachers with ideas. It would make me excited that they were comfortable enough to do that, and they felt empowered to brainstorm to make our school and community better.

One tradition we had was to "roll out the red carpet" for the first day of middle school for the incoming fifth graders. That came about from a former student. He came up to me during an eighth-grade leadership camp right before school started.

Hey Dr. R. I have an idea! When we came up from elementary school, some of us were scared and apprehensive. These eighth graders were big. How about if we roll out the red carpet? We can play loud music. You can announce their names, and we can high five them!

And that is what we did every year on the first day of school. WOW!

Because we were passionate about leadership, it carried over into everything we did. Anything from technology influence to training other schools in leadership. I'm not just talking about the educators but the students as well.

Here is another reflection from a student after she finished her four years of middle school.

Dear Belhaven,
Thank you for a wonderful 4 years. You guys really did a great job preparing me for high school and other obstacles that are waiting for me to come. I will never forget my time at this school because of all the people that I've grown to know and love and all the fun Renaissance events we did. It was such an honor to have the Belhaven Falcon Award to be awarded to me. Thank you because that is something I will never forget. I will make sure that I come back to visit everyone in the school because

they made such a huge impact on my life. I will never forget this school or anyone that taught me.

The following email from a teacher speaks volumes about the climate and culture that can be created and expected when we are all passionate about the success of our students. She understands the value of the "whole person."

You have helped me realize one important thing within myself that before I was not aware...I have to be with people that let me grow --spiritually, mentally and emotionally. Thank you for the opportunities you have created for me to become a better person and most importantly for believing I could. What warms the heart is when you create the opportunity for all of us to become leaders. You allow us to speak what we feel without fear of repercussion. You have integrity and are gifted with the ability to see the possible.

Shift happens.

HOW DO YOU WANT PEOPLE TO TALK ABOUT YOU AT THE DINNER TABLE?

If you are an educator, people are definitely talking about you at the dinner table. You are talking about them, too. Something became apparent in the year 2020. We ate at the dinner table more because the pandemic of 2020 forced us to. That part, I liked.

Many conversations with parents over the years started with, "Last night at dinner, Johnny told us about the fun he had at the pep rally." Or "That STEAM Fair got me thinking about what I really want to do. Maybe, we can get a club to meet after school." Granted, there were negative conversations as well. If you proactively give people something to rave about in the positive realm, the negatives will be dimmed.

One of my goals as a principal was to have more positive contact than negative. If I had a negative phone call, I would make ten positive calls. This proactive approach changed the way people viewed the *Principal's Office*. It became a badge of honor. Instead of *What did I do wrong?* It became, *Can we see Dr. R.?!* WOW! Paradigm shift. That created a whole different dinner table conversation.

The pandemic created a lot of unknowns but it also allowed us the opportunity to do things differently. The people in my circle grasped the moment to fine-tune the quality of what we controlled. How did it change the conversation? Keep expanding your groups of people that make you feel like what you do matters. As you expand your control, you broaden your positive influence.

KEEP A GREAT NEWS FILE

There are days when everything goes great, and then there are those other days when it seems you cannot do enough. That is why I created a Good News File that eventually turned onto the Great News File.

At the end of my first year as principal, I closed the door and took a deep breath. The feeling of being overwhelmed blanketed my entire body. I asked myself if it was worth it.

I walked down the hall to our last Staffulty meeting of the year. One of the first culture shifts in our school was the redesign of the old faculty meeting. It became an event which included *Staffulty of the Month*. It was a mind changer because it created appreciation rather than bureaucracy and tension. People were not in a hurry to leave. They were n a hurry to get there.

When I walked into the meeting, I was handed balloons and Tootsie Roll Pops. The Pops became a staple because I'd started giving them out all the time, a simple gesture that made a big difference. I was read the following:

The entire staffulty of the Belhaven Middle School wishes to take this opportunity to recognize a very special member of our school community. It has been our unbelievable good luck this year to be blessed with an outstanding new principal and friend, Mr. Frank Rudnesky.

Mr. Rudnesky has totally reawakened our school. He has successfully introduced and implemented the Renaissance program. He has the unique gift of making students and staff members feel appreciated and special. His extraordinary leadership skills make people want to work with him and the ideals he values. Mr. Rudnesky comes early, stays late, and puts his heart and soul into making the Belhaven Middle School be all that it can be.

Thank you for your support, Frank. Thank you for all your hard work. Thank you for making us feel appreciated, and thank you for being you.

The Staffulty of the Month Committee would like everyone here to know that Mr. Rudnesky has been nominated for employee of the month over and over and over again.

Frank, your staff feels blessed to have you here, and we hope that you will continue to work your special magic as our principal for many years to come. We think you deserve both the Renaissance Clap and the Power Clap. We have for you today a token of our esteem and appreciation.

Mr. Rudnesky has been nominated for employee of the month because he...
Really cares about the kids and the staff
Follows through on what he says he'll do
Lets staff know that they are appreciated
Has great expectations for Belhaven
Has improved the morale of the staff
Shows concern and compassion for the students
He can usually be found when you need him
Always has a warm hello, a cheery smile, and the time to listen
Participates in the activities he has initiated with the students
Is a voice of reason with the parents
Is a dedicated man with a contagious enthusiasm that has spread throughout our building

Has worked so hard (often against great adversity) and given so much of himself
Has a special magic that he has worked to make Belhaven a great place once again in which to work.

Well needless to say I never looked back and remained principal for the next seventeen years. That letter was the first addition to my Great News File. At the end of each year, I closed my door and read the Great News about our school. I continue to fine-tune the quality of my life and the lives of the people around me.

SUMMARY

Follow your passion. Encourage other people to follow their passions. Amazing outcomes will occur.

CONCLUSION

What is the most powerful thing you can do?

LOVE

Start every day with love and gratitude. See what happens.

Unconditional love and unconditional leadership are a lot alike. Without love there is no leadership. We all have the ability to love. We all have the ability to lead. You may feel that statement is over simplified but if you treat love and leadership like verbs instead of just emotions and nouns, amazing things happen. Raise the bar; set goals; never ask anyone to do something you would not do; lead by example; create a team, think outside the box, empower, have integrity, always treat people better than you want to be treated, and have fun.

When you begin to see yourself differently, you begin to see the world differently. Not only do you see who you are but you see who you can become. Other people see themselves differently because you empower them through your leadership. They believe in themselves because other people believe in them, too.

Once you accept your role as a leader, you need to show people their self-worth. Some people struggle their entire lives because they do not see their importance. When you do not see your connection to the world, you may never reach your potential. The commitment never materializes.

The "what if" needs to be changed to "I am."

I am smart.
I am strong.
I am beautiful.
I am kind.
I am loved.

With love comes fairness, honesty, and integrity. Everyone you meet becomes important because they are important. When you see who you are, you realize your worth to your organization, the community, the world. You become who you want to be instead of who someone else wants you to be.

Leadership becomes a choice. There are qualities and opportunities that some people are born with then there are people that create their own opportunities and make a conscious effort to live that *Fired Up* life. Are you one of those people that take their destiny into their own hands? Start living the *Fired Up* life before your light dims. The decision is yours. It is a choice you need to make every day.

In a successful organization, there has to be more than one leader. Inspiration comes from many sources. Inspiration, love, passion, success, happiness, integrity, kindness, strength, and fun are connected. They are not one-time events. It is these components that will allow an organization to be successful in the long-term.

Understand that the job you will do in ten years may not exist today. Your job title and the name of your organization may be the same. However, change is inevitable. Timeless principles will enable the success of your leadership to evolve and thrive. Technology advances change the world almost daily. We need to embrace the change and think differently to disrupt the status quo.

I am blessed to have two wonderful, amazing daughters and a wife that shows them the strength of women. I reflect on everything from their eyes. How can I make the world a better place for them? As you build relationships, you do not want to let people down. If you become better, they become better.

My gateway to a career was sometimes unclear as I sailed into unfamiliar territories. Since neither one of my parents graduated from high school, education was not a priority in my house. Although they wanted me to be successful, my mother and father did not know how to translate that into reality. There were many experiences from my childhood that carried forward my ability to have common sense about leadership. You, too, will reflect on your life experiences and how they influenced your leadership qualities. It is important to embed the connections in theory.

When I was six, seven, and eight years old, we lived in a low-rise project development. The "projects" are brick apartment buildings that are federally subsidized for low income families. All the apartments look the same on the inside and out. The projects are arranged in a long rectangle to maximize property space. Our building mirrored every other apartment in the projects. We used to watch my dad walk across the courtyard and hitch hike ten miles to work each day. He worked in an auto parts store that was attached to the biggest department store in our area. My mom worked in a print factory that was within walking distance of our house. *Get to work any way you can* was burned in my memory. When you get there, always give your best effort. It's called work ethic.

I had to work many types of jobs over my formative years to have any money at all for needs as well as wants. Many kids miss this opportunity growing up. These opportunities developed a mindset because barriers were turned to opportunities. My leadership qualities and character awareness were born at an early age.

My first year at community college looked like this: forty hours working at a dairy, one night working at a pizzeria, one night working at a bank, four classes. I also played in one basketball league and coached in another. That is not a schedule I would suggest to anyone but it was the path I chose. Although my dots were not yet connected to the importance of leadership in my life, I became cognizant of my choices and how they affected my future. I needed to start making better choices.

I consciously made a decision to move three thousand miles away and attend the University of San Francisco. I worked my way through college with financial aid, scholarships, and working in a magic shop while performing magic on the street. I set goals, made a plan, and pointed my compass in a direction. Upon graduation, I moved back to New Jersey and opened a magic shop on the boardwalk in Wildwood, New Jersey. I studied the art of magic and researched my favorite magicians. Magic became a passion, and I proceeded accordingly with the will to succeed. Although the magic shop was not lucrative in the long run, it was a creative risk that ended with a Houdini act.

> # WE NEED MORE HERETICS, OUTLIERS, AND DISRUPTORS TO CREATE PLACES THAT DO NOT YET EXIST

That is how I found my way as an educator. The magic shop was closed in the winter. I began to substitute teach. A chance conversation with a principal swayed me to my calling: education. I became a teacher, principal, professor and now an author, speaker, consultant, coach, and disruptor. Along the journey, I added a masters and doctorate degree. Education and leadership became passions.

Some people never have the courage to move away from their negative environments, toxic people, or "do whatever it takes." Other people become average even though they are born into a wealth of opportunity.

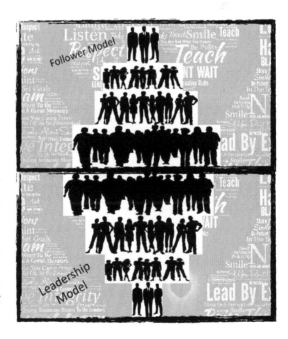

Those new places have always been created. Whether it was a flat world that turned round or a universe that was expanded, paradigms shift. Be ready because it is happening now. Education and leadership must fall into the right hands. It is time to blow up the traditional model and turn it upside down.

LEADERSHIP OPPORTUNITIES EXIST FOR EVERYONE

I fear complacency, isolation, silence, ridicule, mediocrity and bias.

During my last week as principal, a parent asked to speak at an evening celebration. Accomplishments are not possible without a team of stakeholders that accepted their roles as leaders and held our students as first priority. This is her summation of our school.

When I first started to think about what to say tonight, I felt overwhelmed by this daunting task. How could I adequately express gratitude on behalf of all of the parents to this amazing educator for his dedication to our children? Then I remembered a conversation I had with my daughter at the end of the school year and realized in fact SHE had told me what I needed to say. She got into my car after school one day and said, 'I just realized how much of Dr. R is all over our school.' She is entering eighth-grade, and she had just spent the day at Falcon Camp with the fourth graders. She went on to explain that every time she wanted to tell the fourth graders something exciting about Belhaven, she realized it was a 'Dr. R" thing. She and her brother proceeded to list everything that they love about Belhaven including the Renaissance process, the red carpet to welcome the new fifth graders, academic achievement night, the pep rallies, the blue/gold game (of course Dr. R's amazing gold shoes!) and so much more. I have often heard other Linwood children telling incoming Belhaven students about their school. I never heard them say, 'well you know middle school homework is just awesome!' what I hear them talk about are all the Dr. R parts of their school. Every middle school teaches math and science, etc. but Dr. R, you have made it a place where they learn to be leaders, to treat people respectfully and to work their hardest. You have filled our hallways with positive messages and you have always, always put our children first.

As you begin a new phase of your life, I'm sure there are a lot of unknowns for you. There are a lot of unknowns here, too. But what I do know is that while you are relaxing on the beach on the first day of school, the incoming fifth graders will be clapped in on a red carpet, your red carpet. And they will learn about character traits that you've made a vital part of the Belhaven experience. They will read the writing on the walls, and they will grow in an environment created by you. Dr. R, you will always be 'all over our school' and our children who may never know your name will be your students for generations to come.

During my first event as a Belhaven parent, you taught us the nuances of the power clap. Since then, you have continued to educate us. You've reminded us that people will always remember how you made them feel, to express gratitude and appreciation, to 'honk' when you're happy and so much more. Tonight, we would like to express our appreciation by demonstrating your success in educating us. So-if everyone would join me. I think it's time for us to give Dr. R a power clap, triple time.

Thank you, Dr. R for everything. You may be leaving- but your legacy will always be right here, all over our school.

APPENDIX A

INSPIRATIONAL AND FUN IDEAS FROM FIRED UP LEADERSHIP

1. Have a Yearly Theme (Project Rocky, Project Superhero, School Rocks, There Is No Place like Home, etc.)

2. Welcome Forward (Happy New Year)

3. Halfway Celebration (in the middle of the year)

4. Roll out the red carpet (many ways)

5. Start traditions

6. Declare a service-learning platform

7. Yearly Staffulty Picture on the first day

8. Photoshop your head on the shoulders of your favorite superhero

9. Staffulty field trip

10. Tip of the Week

11. Question of the Week

12. Power Clap

13. Secret Handshakes

14. Design, create, trade pins from each yearly theme

15. Create temporary tattoos promoting your theme and organization

16. Renaissance Someone: Student, Staffulty, Parent, Community Member

17. Core Boards - give one, keep one - What's your core word?

18. Pass around a beach ball and marker. Have each person write a power word on the ball.

19. The Starfish Story & other stories of character

20. Paint your walls with murals and quotes

21. Paint your bathrooms with quotes and murals

22. Paint your parking spaces

23. Let your students draw with chalk all around the outside of your school

24. Build A Legacy

25. Leave A Legacy

26. Leave A Legacy and memorialize it on a tile wall

27. Name your hallways

28. Take A Number (Deli Counter Character) with inspirational quotes and actions

29. Put a candy machine in the Staffulty Lounge then give everyone a quarter to use it

30. Put fruit on the counter (5-star check-in)

31. Make your staffulty meeting an event

32. Have an exercise and/or yoga class

33. Spirit Days

34. Have A Leadership Summit

35. Send a thank you note

36. Welcome people on your campus – Greeter/ Tours

37. Brag Board - (hard copy and digital) Brag about your school or organization

38. Make your own inspirational posters with pictures of people you know (students and staffulty)

39. Hold up signs: You Are Awesome! Honk If You're Happy!, Smile, etc.

40. Invite a former student to be a keynote speaker on the first day for staffulty

41. Have Popcorn Paydays

42. Make breakfast for the first ten people at work

43. Buy lunch for someone you rarely see

44. Staffulty of the Month

45. Create the abundance mentality

46. Have a Leadership Exchange (visit another school and have them reciprocate with ideas)

47. Retire a T-Shirt

48. Have a secret pal week

49. Organize a pre-pep rally picnic

50. Have an academic pep rally to celebrate academic excellence, leadership, great character, and participation

51. Create a Great News File

52. Make Positive Contact

53. Have an Ice Cream Social

54. Have A Girls Only Day

55. Have A Guys Night Out

56. People's Choice Awards

57. Leadership Camp for Incoming students (or highest grade) or any stakeholder group

58. Daddy/Daughter Dance

59. Mommy/Son Dance

60. Character Commercials

61. Renaissance Television (RTV)

62. Play music in the cafeteria (have people make different play lists)

63. Play music when people enter your building

64. Dance in the cafeteria during lunch

65. "Dancing with the Staffulty" contest

66. Reward Stamps

67. Pass the Lightsaber

68. Lip Sync Contest

69. Classroom makeover – for staffulty winners or surprises

70. Door decorating contest

71. Blue/Gold Basketball Game - students and staffulty on both teams

72. Dress Down Paydays - for staffulty rewards

73. Penny Wars- for service

74. Make your yearbook an event - no one should be sitting at a desk for their picture, use your yearly theme

75. Almost Anything Goes (AAG) - silly and fun relays for students, parents, and staffulty

76. Pie a teacher, supervisor, or co-worker with shaving cream

77. Staffulty Leadership Relay Olympics

78. Celebrate everyone's birthday on their door and hallway bulletin board

79. Outline the perimeter of your building with American flags to celebrate patriotism

80. Diversity Day - use your imagination

81. Dear You, You Are Amazing! - inspirations that can be torn off a poster (smile, you rock, you are talented, you are beautiful, etc.)

82. Create a Year in Pictures and post to social media

83. Define your organization with ten pictures

84. Stand up on top of your chair or desk and yell: "I am alive!"

85. Collect Smiles

86. Pass Out Smiles (like the free compliments)

87. Make envelopes and write on them, "open when you want to smile." Put things inside that make people smile.

88. Designate a "Friendship Bench"

89. Create a "come sit with me" table

90. Create a "5 Star" restaurant table in the cafeteria

91. Have a guest waiter and waitress dinner

92. Fitness Community Night - fun and diversified

93. Community University

94. BBQ hot dogs and hand them out at dismissal and to people in cars picking up people

95. Meet and Greet Bingo

96. Affirmation Bingo

97. Diversity Bingo

98. TGIM - Thank Goodness It's Monday

99. High Five Friday - with a big spongy hand

100. Icebreakers and team building activities should be a regular part of your repertoire.

APPENDIX B

THE FIVE DOMAINS SUMMARIZED

THE FIRST DOMAIN
SELF - MANAGEMENT AND ORGANIZATION

- Set short term and long term goals and be able to effectively carry the plan to achieve these goals.
    - Write goals for each year
    - Write goals for each week and marking period
    - Develop a personal mission statement

- Work independently and assume responsibility for yourself.
    - Schedule priorities
    - Manage time

- ◆ Understand leadership styles

- Effectively manage your attitude.

- Take creative risks.

THE SECOND DOMAIN
COMMUNICATION AND LISTENING

- Use a variety of written, oral, digital, and nonverbal communication to articulate in a technological, global society.
  - ◆ Improve public speaking skills
    - Infused in curriculum
    - Submit a digital copy in your graduation portfolio
    - Read and/or make a presentation to elementary school, senior citizens, or at a conference
  - ◆ Write a variety of essays
    - Infused in curriculum
    - Submit a digital copy in your graduation portfolio
  - ◆ Convey information properly and timely

- Become an effective listener through authentic listening habits.
  - ◆ Visit and talk to an elementary school and/ or senior citizens

THE THIRD DOMAIN
CRITICAL THINKING, PROBLEM - SOLVING, AND TEAM BUILDING

- Consider different points of view.

- Identify, analyze, and solve problems.
  - ◆ Create an action plan.

- Demonstrate teamwork skills.
  - ◆ Empower others
  - ◆ Travel with your school or other organization
  - ◆ Learn from professionals outside of your school
  - ◆ Participate in a club, sport, school band, and/or community organization
  - ◆ Complete a list of challenges
    - Participate in a Leadership Exchange

THE FOURTH DOMAIN
CHARACTER AND SERVICE

- Demonstrate character traits.

- Complete service.
  - Read to senior citizens and/or children
  - Facilitate your own community service project – "Pay It Forward"
  - Volunteer at a food bank or homeless shelter

THE FIFTH DOMAIN
PASSION

- Follow your passion

- Encourage other people to follow their passions

ABOUT THE AUTHOR

In addition to teaching at the high school and university levels, Dr. Frank Rudnesky was the principal of Belhaven Middle School in Linwood, New Jersey for a span of two decades. During that time, the school was recognized with numerous local, state, and national awards for leadership, technology influence, excellence in performance, and a positive culture. The school was often used as a visitation site for other educators from as far away as Japan.

Frank has developed, implemented, and studied leadership process to enhance organizational culture. He has authored numerous books and articles published in the areas of leadership and technology influence. Dr. R. resides in the Jostens Renaissance Educator Hall of Fame and sits on several non-profit boards including the New Jersey Schools to Watch core team.

Dr. Frank Rudnesky draws on his experience as an accomplished teacher, award-winning middle school principal, and transformational leader to deliver his captivating keynotes and presentations to hundreds of audiences. As you listen to Dr. R.'s style of storytelling and his unconventional journey in life, it will get you *Fired Up* to pursue your passion and empower others to find their passion. His engagement, enthusiasm, and positive energy are contagious.

Frank's education includes a BS from the University of San Francisco, MBA from Rowan University, and a Doctorate from Widener University. He resides in Southern New Jersey with his wife, Dr. Kimberly, two daughters, Franki Maria, Danica Lyn, and their dogs, Maggie and Winnie.

INSPIRE LEADERSHIP

Current Keynotes, Assemblies, Coaching, Consulting, & Workshop topics include:

50 Great Things Leaders Do: Let's Get Fired Up!
Leadership Through Positive Climate and Culture
Live a Fired Up Life with Fired Up Leadership!
Leadership Exchanges
Leadership Summits
Leadership Camps
Student Advocacy and Advisories
Building Relationships and Connections through Leadership
Visible, Tangible, Walkaroundable (V, T, W)
Kindness Is Not a One-Time Event
Customer Service

CONNECT WITH FRANK

 FrankRudnesky@gmail.com

  @DrFrankRud

 www.inspire-leadership.com

CODE BREAKER LEADERSHIP SERIES

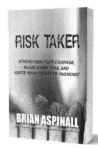

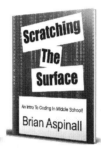

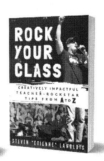

CODE BREAKER KID COLLECTION

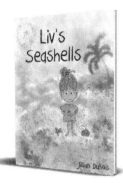

Liv's Seashells

Jillian DuBois

FINDING LOST SMILES

WRITTEN BY VICKIE & DON EPPS

THINK LIKE A CODER!

Deanna Pecaski McLennan &
Brian Aspinall
Illustrated by Alexandria Masse

Gracie

Written by
Daphne McMenemy

Illustrated by
Alexandria Masse

What Happens When I Learn to Code ?

Written by
Daphne McMenemy
& Brian Aspinall

Illustrated by
Daphne McMenemy

Gracie: The Maker

Written by
Daphne McMenemy

Illustrated by
Alexandria Masse

Look for the MATH Around You

PATTERNS

Look for the MATH Around You

GEOMETRY

Look for the MATH Around You

FRACTIONS

ESTIMATION

Look for the MATH Around You

MATH CHATS

Look for the MATH Around You

ARRAYS

Look for the MATH Around You

www.codebreakeredu.com

Made in the USA
Middletown, DE
12 January 2023

21996551R10115